A Winning Combination

A Winning Combination

WRITTEN BY

Dr. Julie Anthony

and

Nick Bollettieri

Charles Scribner's Sons New York

Library of Congress Cataloging in Publication Data
Anthony, Julie.
A winning combination.
Bibliography: p.
Includes index.
1. Tennis for children. I. Bollettieri, Nick,
joint author. II. Title.
GV1001.4.C45A57   796.342'2   80-18095
ISBN 0-684-16710-7

1 3 5 7 9 11 13 15 17 19   F/C   20 18 16 14 12 10 8 6 4 2
Printed in the United States of America

To my parents, Tom and Molly Anthony,
and my husband, Dick Butera
—Julie Anthony

Acknowledgments

I would like to thank Billie Jean King, Tracy Austin, Jeanne Austin, Tony Trabert, Charlie Pasarell, David May, Kathy May, Barbara Jordan, and Ben Testerman for giving us extensive and insightful interviews. I would also like to thank the late Dr. John Marshall, whose help on our physical health chapter was invaluable. We deeply mourn his untimely death. We would also like to thank Walter Iooss for the photos that appear in Chapter 8.

Contents

Preface

A little over a year ago, during a group coaching session with Nick Bollettieri in Sarasota, Florida, I suddenly paused and took note of the other participants on the court. Surrounding us were young people from eleven to seventeen years of age and of varying degrees of talent, competence, and desire, pursuing the same goal—trying to improve their skills in the game of tennis. It occurred to me then that between Nick, one of the nation's top teaching pros, and I, a touring tennis professional and psychologist, we had a vast amount of information about the game that we could impart to these youngsters and, particularly, to their parents.

In the past ten years, tennis has taken on totally new dimensions as a sport, profession, and business, creating many more options for children interested in the game, but also many more dilemmas. Thus, the decision-making process for parents and children has become much more complex. Children, through lack of experience and knowledge, are not always in the best position to make certain judgments for themselves, but sometimes neither are their parents. Why, when, and how should a child start playing tennis? What type of training is necessary? What kind of physical talent is needed? How does tennis affect schoolwork? How can it affect a child's emotional state? What is the best way for a parent, child, and coach to interrelate? All of these questions, and many more, parents must deal with on a daily basis—often without the necessary information and knowledge to make the best decisions for their child.

An important part of being a good parent is knowing

which decisions to make and which to leave up to the child. This book will help parents make tennis-related decisions that, in the long run, will bring happiness and self-fulfillment to their children through the sport. In this context, we are not concerned as much with tennis technique or the mechanics of developing a young tennis player as with the parental art of maximizing the psychological and emotional rewards to a tennis-playing child.

Nick Bollettieri came to tennis relatively late in life but with a background full of experiences in other sports, particularly football. Not until he was a freshman at Spring Hill in Mobile, Alabama, did he take up the game. Teaching himself, he made the tennis team and competed for his college in his sophomore, junior, and senior years. His coaching experience began in 1953 when he was in the army, where he coached the 187th Airborne team until 1957. However, his thoughts for the future did not lie in tennis, but in a career in law. In 1957/1958, while attending Miami Law School, he became the teaching pro in North Miami Beach to make ends meet. It was then that he realized that coaching, rather than law, was his true love in life, and he has remained with that profession ever since. Today, he is the head pro at the Colony Beach and Tennis Resort in Sarasota, Florida; part owner of another club on Longboat Key, Florida; owner of a summer tennis camp in Beaver Dam, Wisconsin; and, most proudly, has a tennis academy for children on Longboat Key. At the academy, fifty or so students (mostly live-in) of all ages and socioeconomic levels, from all over the United States and the world, take regular academic courses but spend most of their free time in an intense tennis program. From this group of hopefuls, young stars have already emerged who have won major junior titles and achieved high rankings at the state and national levels, but who, nevertheless, are treated like everyone else at the academy. From this group of young people, Nick hopes to develop another Brian Gottfried, one of his most prized pupils—honored not only as one of the world's best tennis players, but as one of the most decent, honest, and hard-working human beings he has known. Nick has been personally involved in all aspects of tennis, including being the father of two young tennis-playing girls, and brings to this book experiences as a parent, competitor, and coach. Tennis was just one of many sports I was introduced to as an eight year old growing up in Santa Monica, California, but with me it became a passion. Starting then, in 1956, my daily childhood routine consisted of racing home from school to change and quickly pedaling my bike to the nearest public park to play tennis with anybody I could find until dark. The results of these beginnings have been ten years of junior competition, four years of collegiate competition with Stanford University, and nine years of part- and full-time professional competition. In my years in tennis I've not only seen every kind of tennis talent and parent but have also seen huge changes in the game itself, particularly as it pertains to women. This coincidence of being at the right place at the right time, coupled with my education in clinical psychology, have made me well aware of the psychological demands, sacrifices, stresses, and benefits of growing up with a sport, competing as a child, and participating as an adult woman in the professional world of athletics. Now, as a stepmother to five children who play, I'm experiencing yet another side of the sport—as a parent. Thus, together Nick and I cover the total spectrum of the game and feel our shared knowledge can be extremely helpful to many perplexed children and parents. We also hope the reader will realize that although the emphasis of the book is obviously on tennis, many parts of it transcend any individual sport and apply to the larger subject of relationships between parent, child, and coach.

Julie Anthony

1.

Tennis and children

When seriously considering tennis for a child, it becomes apparent that the game offers much more than just pure physical exercise. Tennis is social, international, relatively inexpensive, accessible, can be played one's whole life for pleasure and fitness, and, for those who are exceptionally talented, it can offer a profession as a teacher, coach, or tournament player.

Social Advantages

Unlike other sports, such as swimming, track, or cycling, which can be enjoyed entirely by oneself, tennis demands at least two people for a game. That is far simpler, however, than putting together a team or squad for soccer or baseball. Moreover, a practice partner can be tall, short, fat, skinny, young, old, rich, poor, male, or female—as long as the ball comes back over the net fairly regularly.

Paradoxically, many parents feel that a child's devotion to tennis is socially constricting. They believe the child is sacrificing more "normal" and important social activities to a simple game that will be of little reward in later life. First, they must understand that the primary goal for any child's playing tennis is to have fun; the secondary goal is to become competent, and, to become good at anything, you have to love it. If you love tennis, it's a privilege to play; therefore, what may seem like a sacrifice to others may be simply a matter of choice. Second, instead of confining a child's social life, tennis opens up an entirely new one—a new set of

5

friends and perhaps travel and exposure to new situations, if the child is good enough to compete.

Furthermore, tennis gives boys and girls the opportunity to develop a natural camaraderie in a relaxed setting, as opposed to the more self-conscious atmosphere of a party or some other prearranged social event. Boys and girls who play tennis become friends and practice partners who share the emotions of working hard and of winning and losing. Their primary orientation is not that of being a boyfriend or girl friend. People united by an outside interest find it easy to establish relaxed and genuine communication. Thus, not only does tennis add a new dimension to a child's social life, it also provides an arena for healthy and open interactions between boys and girls.

When to Start

The first question a parent often asks is, what is the ideal age for a child to start playing? Careful now; ideal age for whom? For the child to start realizing *your* desire to be the parent of a champion? Forget it. Jimmy Connors may have started at two, and Chris Evert Lloyd and Tracy Austin at three, but these people are exceptions and represent an extremely small fraction of the tennis-playing population. The vast majority of children will never win even the smallest local tournament, much less make a name for themselves in the sport, so there is no need for them to begin tennis seriously at such an early age. Besides, starting early is no guarantee of excellence. Perhaps most important, Tracy Austin and Jimmy Connors *wanted* to play tennis at that age; it was *their* strong desire, and not that of their parents, that propelled them into the game.

Once parents are sure that they are introducing their child to tennis for the child's benefit, and not to fulfill the parents' expectations and needs, the ideal age to start is somewhere between eight and eleven years old. Tennis is a complicated skill and, if the child shows a great interest in the sport early on, there will be time for him or her to strive for any goal realistically. Starting even younger than eight is fine, if the child is anxious to do so, but it is doubtful that any advantage will be gained from it.

Athletic Ability

Sadly, many children are never given a chance to learn tennis, because their parents mistakenly believe that athletic ability is a prerequisite for playing and enjoying the game. Of course, physical ability is an asset, but any child can learn the game of tennis and have fun regardless of innate talent. Just as important, natural ability is not fixed for life. It changes, often drastically—and usually for the better—as the individual grows. In fact, tennis can act as a catalyst, providing a child with an enjoyable means of developing physical skills. In short, parents shouldn't trust themselves to judge their child's sports talents unless they are experienced coaches and incredibly objective in their thinking. Finally, even at the highest level of the game, pure athletic ability does not differentiate top players, who must possess a combination of athletic, technical, intellectual, and psychological strength. If a child is weak in one of these areas, he can learn to compensate for it in the others, as most pros have had to do.

How to Start

There are several inexpensive, simple ways a parent can introduce a child to tennis. Until you know that your child is going to like and pursue the game, just borrow a racket for a while. Don't worry about a precise size or type of racket, just something that's not too heavy (generally a 4⅜- to 4½-inch grip size light racket will do). However, do make sure your child has a good pair of tennis shoes (see Chapter 5, on equipment). Next, check your local public park or public recreation commission for any junior tennis programs. These programs are usually free or very inexpensive and offer group instruction. If you belong to a country or tennis club,

7

check there for junior programs. These will probably be more expensive but have smaller groups. In any of these programs your child will be grouped on a court with children of roughly similar skill and age levels and will participate in a lesson of about an hour to an hour and a half in length. Another option, if you have ever played tennis, is to take your child out yourself to hit a few balls. I don't recommend trying to teach your child anything but perhaps the forehand and backhand grips; just give him or her the chance to swing at the ball and make contact sometimes. Remember, you're not a coach, and the object of these first few outings is to see if your child would have any interest in the sport, so make it fun and don't try to teach. At this stage it's not important if your child has the proper strokes. Later on, if he or she shows real interest, you might want to invest in private lessons, discussed in Chapter 7, on coaching.

Sharing Decisions

It's important that the decision to start tennis in earnest be made jointly between parent and child. It may be the parents' money for lessons, rackets, and all the rest, but the child's time and effort will also be invested. Obviously, a parent has more experience, knowledge, and maturity than a child and can help bring out all the possible pros and cons of tennis when discussing the game. A child who wants to play regularly and take lessons from a coach should be made to understand that it takes time and a lot of practice to learn tennis, and on many occasions the game can be very frustrating. The child should also know that in choosing tennis he may have to forfeit other activities. Once a bargain is struck and a commitment is made, parent and child should agree on minimum practice requirements. If the child doesn't follow through, parents should find out why. Perhaps the coach is not the right one, or practice hours might be excessive, there may be too many conflicting activities at school, or the game has simply lost its appeal. Whatever the problem, parents must *listen* to the child, be flexible in their demands, and try to let the child make the final decision.

Too Masculine or Too Feminine?

As for any lingering old-fashioned ideas that tennis is unfeminine for women or sissified for men, forget them. Thanks to the advent of open tennis in 1968 (tournaments allowing professionals *and* amateurs to compete), the rapid growth of the women's professional circuit, tournaments in general, and the excellent exposure tennis has had on television, the sport has become equally attractive to members of both sexes. Also, the desired image now for both men and women is to have healthy, strong, toned bodies, which tennis offers.

Competitiveness

Another matter of concern to parents is the element of competitiveness in tennis. It is commonly thought that a child must be competitive to play because, after all, tennis is basically a contest between at least two people. First, we are all competitive in some sense of the word, even if it's only against ourselves, and that certainly doesn't rule out the enjoyment of hitting tennis balls or the probability of winning matches. As Eric Heiden, Olympic gold medalist in speed skating, says, "When I skate I don't really care if I win or lose, so long as I skate the best I can and set personal records." A child can go out to play and enjoy pitting his talents against those of another child with a goal of winning, or he can go out and enjoy trying to improve some facet of his own game, regardless of the outcome.

Children learn what competition is all about through their parents. If a parent puts a great deal of emphasis on winning at all cost, the child will soon react to this pressure by fearing and avoiding competition. On the other hand, if a parent stresses enjoyment, trying hard, and self-improvement, the child will become positively motivated to compete and will use competition as a measure of his progress. In no way does the enjoyment of competition imply ruthlessness or the negative sense of aggressiveness.

Competitiveness is often linked closely with motivation. In simple terms, children are either motivated to play, practice, and, perhaps, compete or they aren't. If not, the lack of motivation may be due to a genuine dislike for tennis or the result of excessive parental pressure.

Parental Misguidance

The greatest error parents can make is to voice expectations for their child beyond that of having a good time. As soon as a child begins to play for a parent's approval or to maintain harmony in the family, his motivation and fun will diminish instantly, no matter how talented he is. Many young players with potential have been turned off tennis by their parents, and some great talents have been destroyed in this fashion. Unfortunately, among tournament circles one often hears that "Susie has super talent, but her parents put too much pressure on her, and she just gets too uptight and nervous to win."

Parental pressure can take many forms. It can be a question of forcing a child to practice, take lessons, or compete in matches against his will. An insidious byproduct of parental expectations can also be overcriticism of a child's efforts. A child shouldn't be made to feel that every mistake will be thrown back at him. It's hard enough to go through the agony of *playing* badly.

Psychologically, human beings learn just as well, if not more effectively, from positive than negative reinforcement. It is more helpful to tell a child what he did well and suggest what to try in the future than to belabor what went wrong and what not to do. Even on the most disastrous days, something positive can be said, such as, "I guess you didn't play well today, but I liked the way you kept trying," rather than "you really played badly today." A child's coach is responsible for tennis technique, but parents can help his mental well-being.

Making unflattering comparisons between a child and his peers can also be damaging to the child's motivation. Remember that every child is unique and learns at his own pace; each individual's progress is totally unrelated to that of anybody else's and should be gauged only against itself. To better illustrate how parents can influence their child's motivation and liking for the game, Nick tells us about some students he has coached.

I've had a little thirteen-year-old girl in my local program in Sarasota for two years now. When she first came, she was a complete introvert—sour-faced, discontented, moody; she just didn't enjoy anything. No matter what happened on the court, she would always put her head down. Because she was a local girl, her mother was almost always present at her lessons and often came up to me afterward to say, "How in the world can my daughter do so poorly? Look at her out there. All the other kids can hit the ball, but she can only connect maybe once out of ten times!" Riding home in the car she would also impart these thoughts to her daughter. That particular summer the child came alone to my camp in Beaver Dam, Wisconsin. After three weeks we began to make some progress, slowly because she was not a natural athlete, but progress all the same. I made sure always to point out the areas where she had improved and compliment her often on them. Away from her mother, she was not always badgered and reminded of how much better other kids were doing. Instead, at camp she had time to feel good about herself. Now, two years later, this child's personality has changed entirely. She's happy and really enjoys playing tennis. Her skills have improved immensely, and she even plays tournaments and occasionally wins a round or two. As a result of this change in self-esteem she's also doing better in her schoolwork. By the way, her mother and I have had many discussions, and she now comes to the courts infrequently. Today, instead of talking directly to her child, she discusses her thoughts with me, and lets me convey them to her daughter at my own discretion.

To show how the parents' attitude can affect the child in a different, more positive way, another family comes to mind. The situation here is pretty tricky because this family has four children playing tennis, so rivalry among them can get pretty high, and the temptation to make comparisons to each other is strong. In this family of two girls and two boys all are good players, not average, but good. However, each has totally different personal goals in tennis and treats the sport differently. The two older girls could play on any high school or college team, but competition is not their bag. Instead, they keep tennis as a social hobby. The next youngest child, a boy, is just the opposite—competition and winning are everything to him. In fact, this child has the ability to be an outstanding player, but he has to learn to accept losses, to accept them not as defeats in life but as steps in becoming more mentally tough, cutting down on mistakes and building more physical strength. So this child has very high tennis goals and will need his parents' help to channel his intensity and drive into constructive ways to help him achieve those goals. The last child, the youngest, is a boy who, for his very young age, hits the ball quite well. However, he's highly influenced by his brother and sisters' love of the game and really enjoys himself on the court. The amazing thing with this family is how the parents react to each child as an individual and understand that each child has different abilities, desires, and personalities. I have never seen parents more complimentary, more encouraging, and less concerned with winning than these parents. Certainly they would like their children to experience victory, but it's more important to them to see their children progress as good human beings. The point is that these parents are raising happy children who really love tennis, because each child is made to feel proud of his or her own individual accomplishments as they measure up to his or her own goals, not as they compare to anyone else's.

As we said earlier, children change rapidly. Johnnie might be doing something today that allows him to win in the short run, but Susie might be developing skills that will win for her later, in spite of present losses. Thus, comparing Johnnie with Susie would be fruitless, if not harmful. All a child has to know is that, in his parents' opinion, he is the most wonderful tennis player who ever lived. However, parents must ground their comments in reality or else the child will think them too exaggerated and therefore worthless. Helping a child feel proud of his progress without being compared with anyone else will also help the child develop a sense of self-worth. One of the most important ways in which a parent can use tennis, then, is in building a child's self-esteem. He can learn that his feelings of self-worth are not dependent on a tennis score. Values that transcend any sport—honesty, effort, self-reliance—can be stressed, so that any child can feel like a winner regardless of outcome.

The Passion for Tennis

On the other end of the spectrum from the youngsters Nick just described are the children who can't seem to get enough of tennis. They can't wait to get to the courts after school, and they stay there until dinner time. On weekends they're in heaven because they can play all day long. They eat, sleep, and breathe tennis. This enthusiasm should be shared by parents as long as the child does not miss meals, neglect homework, abandon family duties, or become overtired. There are so few times in anyone's life when a person truly falls in love with an activity and becomes dedicated to it that a child should be allowed to pursue this passion, regardless of talent, as long as it absorbs only his leisure time. Let a child follow his heart. Billie Jean King, Rod Laver, Pancho Gonzales, and Margaret Court weren't just luke-

13

warm about tennis, they loved it. Don't misunderstand us: because Susie adores tennis doesn't mean she's going to be the next Billie Jean King. But if she is allowed the freedom to play as though she might be, you can't lose. She will either discover her own limitations or, maybe, become one of those rarities—a great player. In either case she will have the satisfaction of knowing she gave her best and wasn't held back by parental restrictions.

Sometimes children and even adults get carried away with their enthusiasm and play too much, not realizing they are tired, hurt, hungry, or just stale. In such instances a parent should intervene and explain the law of diminishing returns: progress can be slowed or even set back by overdoing it. Every young athlete should be taught that his main asset is his body and it should be treated kindly, with adequate rest, food, and lack of abuse. Unfortunately, it is all too common for a parent or coach to push too hard. This is particularly true with children who show some promise. Therefore, adults should always bear in mind that a child rarely gets burned out of his own accord.

2.

Tennis and a Child's Mental Health

Tennis as a Personality Test

Within the field of psychology there are certain tests that are thought to be able to measure someone's personality to some extent. The Rorschach, or ink blot test, is one such assessment tool. The participant is shown a series of cards upon which are symmetrical ink blot patterns and is asked to describe what he sees. The manner in which he perceives these patterns is thought to reveal something about his personality. What kinds of forms he sees, animal or human, whether he makes a composition out of the whole form or just parts of it, whether he sees something that's commonly seen in a blot or something altogether unusual all give indications of how this person ordinarily perceives and makes sense of his world. The problem with the Rorschach is that it takes people of great expertise and experience in interpreting the test to get reliable, valid results.

In a way, almost anything in life can be used as a Rorschach; one just needs to find the people with the right expertise to make use of the information. Thus, how one goes about doing the weekly grocery shopping, driving a car, or playing tennis are all manifestations of one's personality. Because of our background in tennis, Nick and I can look at someone playing tennis and get a pretty good feel for that person as a human being. Does she go for broke on her shots? Does she lose her temper? Is she patient? Does she give a full-out effort? The answers to these questions and many others can be fitted together to give a full personality profile of that person. Similarly, my optometrist, who does eye therapy primarily for children and athletes, feels he can draw certain conclusions about a person's personality by how he or she reacts to certain eye tests. For example, he found that my peripheral vision was weak, but within a somewhat restricted field of vision my ability to focus and maintain attention on a task was quite strong. He concluded from this and other observations that I'm a detail-oriented thinker who doesn't easily think in terms of broad concepts. He was right. However, there is a "chicken or the egg" question here: Did I do well in school because my constricted vision allowed me to do close work (homework) well, or did spending all that time poring over my books constrict my vision? It's the same time-worn heredity versus environment issue and the answer, which probably lies in both domains, most likely has a great deal to do with timing. There likely were certain "critical" years in childhood in which my field of vision was very malleable and influenced by the type of tasks I did. During these years I probably *learned* to constrict my field of vision in order to do the tasks well (the environmental influence). However, how much my vision constricted and how flexible it was were probably related to heredity.

Tennis and the Formation of Personality

The point we want to make is simply this: In adulthood, tennis may be just a manifestation of someone's personality, but in childhood it may serve to help mold that personality as well as be a manifestation of it. In the formative years of childhood, your child is experiencing critical time periods for many physical and psychological traits, characteristics that can be highly influenced by the tasks your child chooses to do. Tennis for a child becomes much more important than tennis for an adult because the child is learning patterns that will be more or less permanent for the rest of his life. I remember as a fifteen-year-old honor student being complimented by the school principal for my good study habits

16

thinking, "Of course I study that way, it's just like tennis. You have to be organized about your practice, be consistent, and work on weaknesses to do well in tournaments, and you have to do the same thing with homework to do well in tests." It was all quite logical to me. How I approached my hobby, tennis, permeated my whole life and dictated how I approached most everything else.

More important than the establishment of work patterns, how I felt about myself was also being established. How much like a winner I felt had very little to do with actual tennis scores. Rather, the approval I won from my parents for my efforts had everything to do with my feelings of self-worth. It is quite difficult for a child to differentiate between having a bad tennis day, being a bad tennis player, and being a bad person, so when a parent criticizes a child for being a bad player, that child may well feel that the parent thinks *he* is bad. Thus, tennis in childhood can help form later work habits, but much more important, it can help form the elusive quality of self-esteem, and a great deal of that responsibility lies with the parents.

Self-Esteem and Mental Pain

In most discussions of sports and health, the focus is generally on physical injuries and pain. Children are guided by parents into some sports and out of others based on the perceived risks of bodily harm. Seldom do parents stop to think of the mental pain that might be involved with a sport. In tennis, the player is on public display and thus subject to the comments and critiques of any passersby. How these comments affect the child depends on how significant that person is in the life of that child. Obviously, in the majority of cases parental approval or disapproval will have a huge impact on how mentally painful the game will be. Unlike physical pain, which varies from sport to sport, mental pain can be inflicted by parents within the structure of any sport. Also, unlike physical pain, which to a certain extent is an intrinsic part of athletics, the mental pain inflicted on a

17

child by a parent (knowingly or unknowingly) can be avoided entirely.

Mental health, like physical health, is the quality of coping with one's environment in a manner that furthers survival. The keystone of mental health is self-esteem—that belief in one's ability to deal with one's environment in a beneficial manner. Mental health and self-esteem evoke feelings of self-confidence, optimism, security, calmness, and adequacy. However, these feelings are grounded in reality and filtered through one's reason. Reason—the ability of the mind to organize the myriad stimuli perceived by the senses—then is the cornerstone of self-esteem. In other words, mental health is dependent on self-esteem, which in turn, is dependent on reason. For example, a person is mentally healthy to the extent that he has used his reason to help him deal with his environment successfully, thereby giving him a sense of high self-esteem. He can use his reason to analyze situations accurately and to deal with them in a manner beneficial to him. Failure to use one's reason successfully results in the failure to achieve a belief in oneself (that is, high self-esteem), which leaves one with feelings of anxiety, insecurity, self-doubt, and inadequacy. Simply, the failure to use one's reason results in low self-esteem and mental pain.

In different terms, self-esteem is a result of the interaction of three factors: self-image, ideal self-image, and reality. How one regards oneself is not necessarily how one would like to be. For example, I may think I'm a humorous person (self-image), but ideally I may want to be as witty as Johnny Carson (ideal self-image). In other words, my self-image may not coincide exactly with my ideal self-image. The third ingredient, reality, is the feedback one gets from the outside world. I may think I'm a witty person (self-image) and want to be wittier (ideal self-image), but no one laughs at my jokes (reality). How mentally healthy or happy one is depends on how closely one's self-image, ideal image, and reality coincide. If I think I'm hysterically funny, yet no one laughs at my jokes, there is a large discrepancy there that makes me feel uncomfortable and unhappy. If I think that I'm a dull and boring person but would like to be the life of the party, another big discrepancy exists that would make me unhappy. These discrepancies are at the root of mental pain.

Learning Fear of Failure

When a child is born there is no discrepancy between self-image and ideal image; that child doesn't know he or she is anything less than perfect. A child is not born with a yardstick against which he can measure himself, he must learn it. Soon the child learns from his parents' approval or disapproval what things he can do to be called good or bad. How many of his actions fall into the "good" category and how many into the "bad" help determine his overall feelings of self-worth. Through this system of parental approval or disapproval, a child's behavior is shaped into patterns that parents find acceptable. By the way, disapproval or punishment encompasses many things in the realm of social learning. It may be a slap or a spanking, a verbal scolding, a reproachful look or frown, or just the absence of any attention at all. If a child (consciously or unconsciously) feels that the chances of being praised or rewarded for an action are high, that child will be eager to try new things in life, that is, he will expect success and be highly motivated. On the other hand, if a child experiences more punishments than rewards, he will expect failure and soon learn to limit his chances of being punished, that is, stop doing things. In this manner a child learns the fear of failure.

Reactions to Fear

Independent human beings generally choose to avoid tasks they expect to fail in. However, sometimes children aren't given this freedom and are forced to do things they fear. Fear is not all bad, though. A little bit of fear, or nerves, can prime an organism for action and make it more efficient physically to fight or flee. More than this moderate amount of fear can hinder action and, taken to the extreme, cause the organism to freeze. The term *frozen with fear* is not figurative, but very descriptive of a real phenomenon. When an organism is scared to an extreme level, certain body functions just shut down, rendering the organism somewhat helpless. A woman can be so scared that she can't scream, or a man can be so frightened that he finds he can't move his legs. Moderately high fear levels in humans can cause such things as slower muscular reaction times, less endurance, and constriction of the field of vision. Thus, a person who is overly anxious or frightened is less sensitive to his environment and less capable of reacting to it, so to force a child to do something he truly fears is almost to guarantee failure for that child. Not only will the child be mentally convinced he will fail, but the fear-induced physiological changes will help bring about that failure.

Fear of Losing

By now you might be wondering if you picked up a book off the psychology shelf instead of the tennis shelf. What does all this have to do with a child and tennis? Quite simply, to ensure happiness for a child in tennis, parents must not instill the fear of failure in the child. In tennis this means *don't make a child afraid to lose.* In losing a tennis game, a child should never feel that he has failed or is a failure. This feeling of failure can lead only to anxiety and avoidance of the sport. The greatest motivating force in Chris Evert Lloyd's tennis career was her father, Jimmy Evert, who also coached her. "I think there was just one big reason for why I wanted to play tennis, and why I put all the work into it— for my father. I played tennis for my father." Mr. Evert's advice to his daughter was, "Don't be afraid to lose. Losing is no crime." Another parent with similar advice was Jeanne Austin, Tracy's mother. Tracy relates her mother's philosophy:

> You know, my mom always said that sometimes a loss might be better than a win because if you win, you think

everything's going fine and you just go and practice la-dee-dah, and you don't practice anything special. If you lose, you practice harder, and you practice on something that obviously was a weakness.

A player with a different relationship with his father is Billy Martin. Considered to have had a very bright future after a spectacular junior career, Martin fell into obscurity in the pros. Although he certainly gains gratification from the game, having stayed in it for as long as he has, some peers like Harold Solomon feel Martin's father pushed him too hard. When Billy was younger and showing some potential, Mr. Martin moved his family to California for his son to be in a better tennis environment. Solomon commented, "Billy had all his eggs in one basket. When all you have is tennis, life is just survival. You lose perspective, and the pressure becomes incredible." As Peter Bodo pointed out in an article on Martin,* in the pro circuit, "Bad results aggravated the father's anxieties. . . . It got to the point where Martin, a qualifier at Palm Springs in February 1979, asked his father not to attend the tournament. . . . 'I've just asked dad to sit in the background,' Martin said. 'I still want to do well for my parents—prove that it wasn't all a waste of their time and effort.' " Martin has said, "There wasn't much sympathy except from maybe my mom. My dad, he's not the kind of guy who hands out sympathy easily." Even at twenty-two, Martin would still like his parents' approval. One detects in him a note of sadness and alienation from his father, and ultimate failure to please him. I'm sure Mr. Martin acted only out of the best intentions and love for his son, but by having too narrow expectations and ideas of success, he damaged his relationship with Billy. Billy's fear of losing and its subsequent punishment (that is, lack of sympathy) from his father was exemplified by his asking Mr. Martin not to be present at his matches in Palm Springs. In order to

*"What Happened to Boy Wonder Billy Martin?" in *Tennis* Magazine, May 1970.

avoid punishment, Billy had two choices: stop playing, or not play in front of his father; he chose the latter. Most children under similar circumstances would choose to give up tennis, which is how more great talent is wasted than by any other way.

How Parents Instill the Fear of Losing

Larry Willens, a physical education instructor at San Diego State and a tennis coach in the San Diego area, discusses the role of parents in tennis.

Out of the hundreds of juniors in San Diego, one or two will be successful as pros. Part of the reason the percentage of successful players is so low is "tennis parents." It is rare when the national 12 or 14 champion makes it later on in his or her career.

By the time the 12s and 14s get out of the juniors, they have been "beaten" so much by parents they hate the game. By beaten, I don't mean physically beaten, although this happens too often, but mentally beaten, which is much more harmful. Tennis players play either to win or to not lose. Too many juniors play to not lose. In fact, these kids are scared to death to lose. After a match they know they are going to hear, "How did you do? Did you win? You should have hit your forehand crosscourt. How could you lose to her?" The list of comments goes on and on.

When I talk about the fear of losing, we must realize it is not the loss the player fears, but how he or she feels others will react.

Thus, you can see how parents, through certain comments, can instill fear in their children. This is not to say that the subject of tennis is off-limits for parents, but they should just be more aware of the subtle messages they may be conveying. For example, if a daughter loses, a parent may not criticize her directly for losing; in fact, the parent is sympathetic. However, he might make excuses to others for her loss: "She's been studying too hard and not practicing; the other girl cheated; she doesn't feel well; she has a sore toe," and so on. The underlying message is that losing is wrong and shameful, for which there must be an explanation, because one's daughter doesn't or shouldn't lose. Actually, what really happened is the daughter got beaten by someone who was better that day—an event, like it or not, that happens many, many times in a player's career, and the parent couldn't cope with the loss. Coming home from practice a child should never be asked, "Did you win?" but rather, "Did you have fun?" Billie Jean King remembers, "My parents never asked me if I won or lost when I came home from practice. They just wanted to know if I had fun." In this way Billie Jean felt no pressure always to win for her parents' approval and love, and felt free to experiment and explore in practice in order to develop new shots at the risk of sometimes losing. Questions like, "Are you happy with the way you played? What would you like to have done better? Did you try anything new?" enable the parent to show interest without putting any value judgment on the outcome.

Confusing Identities

At times it's necessary for parents to sit back and reassess their own attitudes regarding winning and losing. The fear of losing does not just appear in a person miraculously but is usually conveyed from parent to child. Parents, in their earnest interest and involvement in their children, will often confuse their identities with their children's. When the child wins a match, the parent glows with victory and feelings of superiority over other parents. When the child loses, it's the parents' personal defeat. Of course, these parents would never think that this behavior is typical of them—they just "know" that winning makes their children happy, and they are feeling happy or sad only for their children, not themselves. These parents have involved themselves so deeply in their children's lives that they have lost perspective about what makes them happy and what makes their children happy. They have confused their identity with their

23

children's. What might make the child happy is going out and playing tennis; what the parent might think makes the child happy is going out and winning. If the child then feels that he cannot be as much of a winner as the parent would like, the child feels inadequate.

The crux of this problem is the parents' own low self-esteem. A father might think less of himself because he never was the athlete he would have liked to have been. To fill this void in his own psyche, he encourages his son to play sports and puts an inordinate emphasis on winning. With each sports victory, the father imagines it's a confirmation of his own athletic ability, an ability that would have blossomed if only his own father had taken the same interest. A son can only win infrequently for a father like this, with the result that the son ultimately feels that he has failed and is a failure. Low self-esteem has begotten low self-esteem.

The Success Cycle

So far we have looked at some mentally unhealthy ways in which parents can deal with tennis. Now we'll look at the other side to see how feelings of high self-worth and confidence can be instilled in a child through tennis.

Parents have within their power the ability to start their children on a life-long success cycle. What we mean by the success cycle is this: a child can learn to expect positive reinforcement (rewards) for his sincere efforts at any task; this expectation of reward (success) will encourage him to try new things and extend himself to strive for new heights toward self-improvement. Given this confidence, a child's chances for success are increased; thus, success feeds on success.

How this success cycle can be initiated through tennis involves three factors. First, parents should understand their child's goals—listen to him and understand what he wants out of tennis. In this way a parent won't confuse his goals and identity with that of the child. Second, a parent's superior experience and knowledge should be used to point out to

24

the child the many ways of succeeding in tennis. How hard one tries, how sportsmanlike one is, how brave one is in attempting new methods are all yardsticks for success, not just the final score. Parents can help a child focus on some of these areas and lavish praise where it is appropriate, thereby teaching the child that tennis is much more than a score. Third, parents must realize that they are models for a child's behavior. A child learns his attitudes from his parents. How parents react to the child's wins and losses is more important than the child's own reactions. If a child loses a game but is praised for giving a full effort, then he soon learns that it's not a catastrophe to lose as long as one gives one's best. Remember that a parent's reactions to a child's tennis game and even the parent's own behavior on a tennis court are extremely important elements in forming a child's attitudes.

Goal Clarity

Larry Stanley, a tennis pro in Modesto, California, started teaching his son, Randy, when he was two. "My intention wasn't for him to be the best tennis player in the world. It was to begin him early to learn a hand–eye coordinated movement and to have fun. He was eager to learn. Now he's four and he holds the racket, turns, strokes and knows the terminology. We have fun together." Mr. Stanley obviously set attainable goals for his son, that is, tracking a ball with his eyes and hand and having fun. Randy in reaching these goals was having fun, was eager to continue, and has plenty of room to establish his own goals. At Randy's young age it is doubtful that he was able to articulate specific goals, but the goals set by his father were very broad and within his reach. More important, the main objective was to have fun.

An older child will be able to form his or her own objectives, which a parent will usually never know except by asking and *listening*. Some children will have clear goals, but most will not. Parents can then be helpful by explaining to their child that it's much easier to strive for something if one has a clear mental picture of the desired end result. Parents can help their child focus on short- and long-term goals by asking questions like, "Do you want to play tennis for a long time? Do you want to be able to play with your friends? Do you want to play on your school team? Do you want to play tournaments? Do you want to be really good?" Parents should impress upon their child the fact that there are no right or wrong answers to these questions, but that they are just trying to find out his feelings about tennis. Dr. Thomas Tutko, a sports psychologist, advises, "You can teach your child tennis or any sport as long as you remember it's a game and not an extension of the parent-child discipline you're involved in every day. It's got to be a two-way street. Listen to the kid too. That will reduce tension." * Arthur Ashe has this to add: "Some parents want to send their child to a tennis program that stresses results, i.e., that makes the child a winner. If that's what the child wants too—to be a champion—nothing's wrong with that. But we can't all be champions and that's why it's important to teach a child the joy and fun of tennis first, and let the winning take care of itself."

Measures of Success

There are two kinds of successes a child can experience on a tennis court: tennis successes and living successes. It's important that a child enjoy both types. Parents have a great deal of control over the living successes their child experiences because they dole out the social reinforcements or rewards. It is here where the value system of parents comes into play. The type of character traits they admire they will encourage, and the traits they dislike they will discourage. Possible traits parents may want to reward are trying hard, having a positive attitude, thinking well (staying cool under

*Carol Kleiman and Russell F. Stephens, Jr., *You Can Teach Your Child Tennis.* New York: Popular Library, 1979.

pressure), being a good sport, concentrating well, and experimenting with newly taught techniques or strategies. Behaviors parents may want to discourage are extreme displays of temper, cheating, giving up, and excuse making.

Among tennis successes the most obvious one is to win. We're not going to downplay the satisfaction of winning—there's nothing quite like it. Whenever two opposing sides enter into a competition, it's always nice to come out the winner. Unfortunately, half the people who play a tennis match on any given day are losers. Does this make them failures? No! The important matter for a child is that he feel like a winner in his parents' eyes regardless of the score. There are any number of tennis-related things parents can compliment a child on, such as how well a certain stroke was hit, how well a certain point or game was played, how much improvement has been made, or how good his footwork was. In this way a child can understand that tennis is a learning process, win or lose, and many other things besides the score are important.

How should parents reward and punish a certain behavior? We touched on this subject earlier, but it is of such importance that we want now to discuss it further. It is our belief that positive reinforcement or reward is a powerful and safe teaching tool. In psychology it is known that positive reinforcement is as equally effective a training device as negative reinforcement, i.e., punishment. For example, in teaching a daughter to shake hands with adults, it's just as productive to praise her each time she does it as it is to scold her each time she forgets to do so. Both are equally effective in training the behavior, but when negative reinforcement is used, a certain amount of anxiety will accompany the daughter's newly acquired behavior. This anxiety and negative reinforcement have their places. If a parent catches his son playing with matches, a severe scolding or spanking might be in order. Not only do parents not want him to play with matches, but they may also want him to be a bit afraid of them. However, to use negative reinforcement for behaviors where fear is not helpful for a child's survival seems inappropriate to us. An example of how positive reinforcement can be used was related by the tennis great Tony Trabert.

I remember my dad saying to us when we were fairly young that if none of us smoked until we were 21, he'd give us each $500 and that sounded like $5 million. He didn't say, "If I catch you smoking, I'll beat the heck out of you." As a result, none of us smoked and none of us asked for the money because by the time we got to be 21, we realized what a favor he'd done for us.

Thus, we stress the use of a great deal of positive reinforcement—positive reinforcement firmly grounded in reality. A child can quickly sense when praise is insincere or unrealistically given, which may have a backlash effect.

Nick's daughters, Danielle, nine, and Angel, seven, started playing when they were five and four. "I didn't decide they should play tennis; they became interested on their own because they were always around the courts where I am." Nick had two potential problems: trying to teach his own children, and trying to prevent sibling rivalry. He prevented both problems by giving abundant positive reinforcement to each girl for her own individual merits. Whether Nick is on the court teaching his daughters or his other pupils, children and adults, one constantly hears words of encouragement: "Fine! Good! Excellent!" Corrections are given by saying, "That was fine, but I want you to try it this way next time." Nick stresses the fact that he never compares his daughters with each other, or for that matter any player with another player. "I don't think you can be lavish enough with praise, but it must be well thought out. I keep a progress chart on each child and I always finish the lesson when they are having fun and don't want to stop."

Parents as Role Models

Have you ever noticed how much children will mimic their parents? A daughter will walk like her mother, a son will have certain mannerisms exactly like his father's. When I was very young, I often admired my architect father's blueprints. Today, my printing is almost identical to my father's. These are just a few of the more visible ways children will pattern their behavior after their parents. However, there are many more less tangible ways in which children copy their parents. Thus, parents are ineluctably thrust into the role of model for their children. Dr. Benjamin Garber, a psychoanalyst and child psychiatrist on the faculty of the Chicago Institute for Psychoanalysis, cautions:

> Your children learn from you and your reactions, whether you want them to or not. What really happens is that children learn not just a sport, but values, reactions and approaches to life, not just from the game of tennis, but from their parents too.*

If a parent's reactions to a child's wins and losses are positive, then most likely his reactions will be positive also. If a parent responds to a child's loss with a disappointed, "That's okay, dear," the stronger message will be the one conveyed by the tone of voice rather than the words, leaving the child with a sense of failure. In order for a child to gain a healthy mental attitude toward tennis, it is necessary for parents to make a close assessment of their own attitudes. They must make sure they keep tennis as a game in perspective and the nurturing of their child's self-esteem in the forefront.

Tennis is the sport, but self-esteem is the name of the game. Through tennis a child can learn lifetime values, attitudes, approaches to life, and most important, self-esteem. How your child develops as a tennis player is for the most part dependent on factors outside your influence. How much

*Carol Kleiman and Russell F. Stephens, Jr., *You Can Teach Your Child Tennis.* New York: Popular Library, 1979.

natural physical and mental ability for tennis a child has, as well as desire, are largely beyond a parent's control. Definitely within a parent's sphere of influence is how the child develops as a human being. Whether or not a child feels like a success in life, confident in his endeavors, and motivated to explore new areas is powerfully affected by how a parent interacts with his child and his activities.

3.

Tennis and a Child's Physical Health

Some common questions parents have are: Is tennis healthy for my child? How hard should my child work physically? Can my child work too hard? Must he be physically fit even to start playing? Can my child get injured? Should he go on a conditioning program? The answers to these questions vary greatly according to the individual child and his goals for himself.

Is the Child Strong Enough?

Tennis is just a formal extension of play, what a child does anyway. Dr. Ernst van Aaken, a specialist in sports medicine and children, spoke in 1976 to a Road Runner's Club in New York City. He said that "a child is born a long-distance runner, his play is running, and innumerable X-ray exams have demonstrated that the heart of a child has a more favorable volume relative to body weight than adults." He went on to say that the play of children is really a long-distance run interrupted by several breaks. By actually measuring the total distance covered by a seven-year-old boy at play, Dr. van Aaken found that the child covered 5 miles in 90 minutes, taking 400 breaks!* Thus, if a child is a normal, healthy one with no special medical problems, tennis could only add to his good health. On the other hand, even if a child does have certain health problems, with a

*Bob Glover and Jack Shepherd, *The Runner's Handbook*. New York: Penguin Books, 1978, p. 140.

31

doctor's guidance he may still use tennis for rehabilitation purposes.

The Sickly Child

Today, Charlie Pasarell from Santurce, Puerto Rico, can look back on twenty-five-plus years as a highly esteemed world-class tennis professional. He has played in Davis Cup competition for the United States and has won five U.S. men's titles and five U.S. junior titles. However, at the age of three, stricken with polio and wearing leg braces, neither Pasarell nor his parents could ever have imagined he would become an eminent professional athlete. Although his parents were not sure of his future recovery, they never treated him as handicapped, and Charlie never considered himself unable to participate in any children's activities. Only in retrospect did he realize that polio left him with a certain clumsiness in his youth which, with hard work, he was able to overcome.

From the ages of three to five, Charlie had polio, which caused deformities in his leg bones, leaving them somewhat bowed, crooked, and weak. Before he ever played tennis, he was well acquainted with many rehabilitation exercises, which his parents helped him do religiously. Mr. and Mrs. Pasarell, quality tennis players themselves, also encouraged him to start playing tennis to help further his physical development. Charlie attributes his exercises with weights under the guidance of therapist George Johnson, his tennis under the guidance of Welby van Horn, and the inspiration of certain other handicapped children with his total rehabilitation. Charlie remembers:

One of the other kids I grew up with had a very severe case of cerebral palsy. His name was Josito Brandy, and when he first started tennis at eight years old when I first met him, he had a tough time even bouncing a tennis ball and catching it, and a terrible speech problem. Welby van Horn, who was a very great, patient teacher, began by simply rolling a tennis ball to Josito to see if he could trap it and roll it back—and he had a difficult time even doing that. By the time he was fifteen years old he was ranked in the top ten in the U.S. for his age group, and now he's a teaching pro in Puerto Rico. Josito, myself, and a couple other guys used to spend a lot of time just working out, running on the beach, doing exercises, and playing tennis. The fact that he was more handicapped than any of us used to be a tremendous source of encouragement. I used to see him get up and do exercises and then I would do them—I'd feel guilty if I didn't do everything he did. So I had a lot of practice. My parents encouraged me, and the fact that I had friends, like Joe, hard-working guys who loved to do the things I also loved to do, helped me overcome any physical limitations I had.

Alan Finn, twenty-four, of Boston is a fully accredited tennis professional. He is also a victim of cerebral palsy, which has left him with limited use of his right arm and leg. Despite this obstacle, he has acquired quite a formidable record. He was the number-one player on his high school team and went on to New England College to place No. 7 in 1975. He then turned pro, transferred to Northeastern University in Boston (where he graduated with a B.S. in education), and has specialized since in teaching tennis to handicapped youngsters. In addition, last year he was a top-tenner on the New England Grand Prix tournament circuit for teaching pros. Finn explained to *Tennis* Magazine (July 1979) how he's able to play.

I have solid ground strokes, solid volleys. I can cover the entire court well. I might have a little trouble with a leaping overhead, or bending for a drop shot, but these are little things that I can overcome. My only real problem is my serve. I have to toss the ball into the air and then swing at it in the same motion, using only my left arm. It's a weak serve for a pro, relatively speaking, but it's pretty strong for anyone else.

Alan's parents started him playing tennis when he was eleven ("so I wouldn't be sorry for myself"), and he had the motivation to keep at it to prove that "tennis is one sport where someone with a little inconvenience can still participate." As a teacher of handicapped children he says:

> I'm not going to get a multiply handicapped kid on court and tell him, "You're going to play like Billie Jean King or somebody." But I can tell him, "You'll learn how to serve, hit a forehand, a backhand, and learn to volley." I don't stress competition, but a way of getting kids out of the house, to build their self-confidence and give them an immediate feedback of success. You've got to raise children like that in a normal environment, where they can fall down and pick themselves back up. They don't break.

Fatigue

The most important goal for all people is to establish and maintain good health, and, as can be seen from these case studies, tennis is an ideal vehicle by which to learn and achieve the major principles of health. Through tennis a child can learn about such things as conditioning, nutrition, sleep, fatigue, and pain, and how they are all interrelated. A parent's job is to try to help a child become more aware of his body and its requirements for optimal performance. Parents can't feel how tired or hungry their child is, but they can always discuss these matters with him to help him make rational decisions. Children and adults have pretty accurate bodily self-regulators, but they sometimes forget to take the time to attend to them. Barry Geisler, who, as Age-Group Chairman for the National Road Runner's Club, directs twenty-eight weekend age-group running meets a year in New York, stresses that "the body has just so much energy. When more is needed during growth stages, less will be available for running, and performance is affected."* This

*Bob Glover and Jack Shepherd, *The Runner's Handbook.* New York: Penguin Books, 1978, p. 142.

explains not only how a child's body automatically regulates itself, but why his performance may be inexplicably erratic at times. Thus, fatigue is part of life, a part of sports, and is nothing to be afraid of or avoided, especially in children. The body can take a lot more than you think. In fact, performing until fatigue sets in will gradually increase endurance and have certain beneficial physiological effects. Playing in a state of semitiredness conditions the body to process oxygen more efficiently. Arteries and capillaries open for better circulation, and the number of capillaries in the heart and skeletal muscles increase and bring even more oxygen to the heart and muscles, helping remove waste products.

Fatigue as a Mental Toughener

Fatigue can also be a psychological teacher. A child can learn that fatigue need not be an impassable barrier, but only an obstacle that can indeed be overcome. This isn't a bad lesson to learn for life in general. In practice or in a match, children can learn that even though they think they are dead tired, they can still put out a little more, and in a match this could be the difference between winning and losing. To win a practice game or match when exhausted is a huge confidence builder. Then they can feel proud because they conquered two opponents, the other person and their own fatigue. Their mental endurance has affected their physical endurance, and perhaps they have gained insight into the capabilities of their mind to expand their limitations. This lesson is best left to a coach to teach rather than a parent. A coach who is experienced in teaching children is more knowledgeable about how far they can be pushed. Also, sometimes to elicit the maximum performance out of a child, a coach has to be a bit of a Simon Legree, a role we don't see as beneficial for a parent. It is psychologically much healthier for a child if he just has pleasant, fun, and loving associations with you and tennis. Parents should leave the drill sergeant routine for a qualified coach.

Limitations

There are, however, limits to the beneficial effects of fatigue. Although it is difficult to talk definitively on this subject because much has to be learned through trial and error, what is important is that a child learn to listen to his own body and try to differentiate between enough and too much. In very general terms, if a child is not recovering from hard practice sessions by the next day, if he is irritable at night, or showing a loss of appetite, then an enforced day or two of rest might be necessary, as well as an easing up of his tennis program. Fatigue can also involve more of a mental staleness than a physical weariness, for which the remedy is the same: a few days totally away from tennis. It's important to remind the child who has a tendency to overwork that the quality of practice is more significant than the quantity. One hour of efficient, ordered practice is much more valuable than three hours of fatigued, sloppy, or haphazard practice. The overworker may have to be forced to rest sometimes, but after experiencing renewed energy and freshness as a result of these rests, he will soon learn to pace himself better.

Experiencing Pain

Pain is certainly not a dominant feature of tennis, but it is not an uncommon one either, and it is sometimes necessary for further development in the sport. Before parents get alarmed about the physical safety of a tennis-playing child, they should think about the alternatives to being active. Yes, a child may have to suffer the discomfort of a blister, but isn't that preferable to the longer-term discomforts of being overweight, unenergetic, weak, or generally not in the best of health? Of course, the more active a child is, the more vulnerable he will be to injuries, but in tennis these injuries are usually minor and can often be avoided with proper training.

Seven Reasons Why a Child Can Get Hurt

There are many reasons why a child can get hurt, but we have found most of them to fall in certain general categories. In *The Runner's Handbook,* Bob Glover and Jack Shepherd list ten reasons why runners get injured. Seven of these reasons apply particularly to tennis players.

1. *Poor flexibility* Muscles that are tight are much more prone to injury than ones that are stretched. Although most children are inherently flexible because their body tissue is highly elastic, a program of stretching exercises (see Chapter 4 on conditioning) is highly recommended for all players, young and old.
2. *Stress and tension* The nervousness associated with any competitive sport can cause muscles to tighten and become less flexible, leaving them susceptible to injury. Again, stretching exercises can induce relaxation and alleviate this problem.
3. *Overuse* Playing too much, as a result of a child's high motivation (or a parent's or coach's overdemands) can lead to musculoskeletal injuries. If a child seems to lack his usual energy, is catching cold frequently, or having a number of physical complaints, a few days' rest are in order before a more serious injury ensues.
4. *Improper training* Improper training can lead to injuries such as tendinitis, especially of the elbow. Also, any drastic changes in a training schedule can cause injuries. If a child is going to increase his or her training program or change court surfaces, it should be done gradually.
5. *Injury rehabilitation* After an injury has been incurred, it becomes extremely important to make a slow reentry into tennis. Not only has the injured area been weakened, but so have the surrounding muscles, and both areas must be gradually strengthened.
6. *Improper equipment* Poorly fitting shoes can cause a number of foot, ankle, and leg problems. Rackets with

37

grips too large or too small, and that vibrate too much on ball contact, can cause arm problems. (See Chapter 5 for a further discussion of equipment.)

7. *Poor advice* When an injury has occurred, it is extremely important that it be taken care of by a qualified person. The area of sports medicine is a specialty with which not all medical doctors are familiar. Choose a doctor who primarily deals with sports injuries and who, preferably, is an athlete as well.

Common Tennis Ailments

As closely as you may heed the advice just given, injuries may occur. The following is a list of the most common problems with some practical suggestions from a layman's (albeit experienced) point of view on how to cope with them.

Blisters

Quite simply, blisters are caused by friction. Shoes that are too tight or too loose, wet socks, folds in socks, heavy threading in shoes, hot pavement, and many other things can cause blisters on the feet. In addition to wearing properly fitting socks and shoes with good thick soles, wearing two pairs of socks can be helpful in preventing blisters. Rubbing vaseline or lanolin on a child's feet before he puts on his shoes will also help avert or alleviate the problem. Blisters occur on the hands because of improper grip size or a change in the manner of gripping the racket. When children are first starting out in tennis, their hands and feet have not developed the callouses that will later protect them from the wear and tear of the court. Therefore, particularly at the beginning, be on the lookout for blisters.

As soon as your child feels any kind of chafing, he should stop and apply a Band-aid or adhesive tape to the area before a full blister develops. Because feet and hands perspire so much, the area should be thoroughly dried and tincture of benzoin applied to toughen the skin and help the Band-aid stick. If you have a full-fledged nasty blister, puncture it with a sterile needle and drain it, then apply tincture of benzoin, which will sting this time. Next, apply a Band-aid or gauze and then Dr. Scholl's mole skin, which is a sort of felt Band-aid that, because of its thickness, offers great protection and comfort. In some cases for blisters on the hand, a glove might be the best remedy. In fact, some professional players like Cliff Drysdale always wear a glove.

Tennis elbow and tendinitis

Fortunately, children do not tend to get tennis elbow, which seems to be much more a problem of middle-age or professional players. However, because it does occur in tennis, it's best that parents know something about it, in order to help prevent their child from ever getting it. Tendinitis occurs when the tissue connecting muscle to bone (the tendon) becomes torn and results in inflammation and pain to that region. When this happens to the elbow, it's called tennis elbow.

Dr. John Marshall, who was director of sports medicine at the Hospital for Special Surgery in New York, described tennis elbow as being the result of the "overload phenomenon." According to this concept, tennis elbow arises from excessive wrist action. The muscles that power the wrist originate at the elbow and are the muscles that get injured. Thus, excessive wrist action is generally the cause of tennis elbow, especially if the contact of racket and ball is behind the player's body, putting the entire force of the stroke on the arm. Also, hitting a ball hard off-center can cause a great deal of racket vibration and arm stress, resulting in torn tendons. These stresses are more likely to occur at the beginning of a game, before the arm muscles have had a chance to warm up fully. Players are especially vulnerable on cold days. Overuse is another common cause of tennis elbow, which often occurs with professional players. Generally, the player has invited catastrophe by flagrantly abusing his elbow by practicing too much. For example, a zealous player may practice his serve for an hour, drill for an hour or two, and then play two or three sets. Clearly, this routine could cause muscle fatigue and open the door to any number of problems.

A child can prevent tennis elbow by warming up on the court gradually and completely before starting to play hard. He should pay close attention to swinging easily and making contact in front of the body. Hitting the ball hard on any stroke should be attempted only after he is loose and fully warmed up (after about 10 or 15 minutes). Muscle-strengthening exercises can also prevent and help the condition, since strong forearm muscles lessen one's vulnerability. The classic exercise is squeezing a tennis ball or wrist-strengthening device repeatedly.

If a child has developed a case of tennis elbow or tendinitis of any kind, rest is the number-one choice of treatment in the initial stages, but then a graduated program of arm-strengthening exercises should begin. Dr. Marshall recommends for the acute phases of tennis elbow what he calls the RICE treatment—rest, ice, compression, and elevation—a standard treatment for most sports injuries.

With tennis elbow, however, compression and elevation are the least important. Ice should be applied at least once a day, preferably twice, for 20 minutes. Compression is usually for muscle injuries, where the muscle is wrapped with an Ace bandage to keep the swelling down. Aspirin can also be quite helpful to alleviate pain and swelling.

Once the symptoms have disappeared, a child should be very careful to rehabilitate the arm properly. Arm-strengthening exercises should be done for about a week. When the arm has regained some of its strength and there is absolutely no pain, then the child can start hitting the ball easily for about half an hour. This routine should be increased very gradually and stopped immediately if there is a recurrence of any pain. Most important, a child should go to the crux of the problem and improve his hitting technique. The technical points that should be stressed are hitting the ball in front of the body, leading with the racket, wrist, and arm—not the elbow—on the backhand, and avoiding excessive wrist action in hitting topspin. Dr. Marshall also recommends that a medium-stiff aluminum racket, strung at 55 pounds of tension, be used.

We don't feel that any child's tennis career is more important than his health, nor do we feel that even if your child is a highly motivated prodigy he should risk future development by trying to play with an injury. No junior program or tournament is that important. However, for those children who are unstoppable and will not wait for complete recovery, we also have a few reluctant suggestions. Warm the elbow before playing by either soaking it in hot water or using a heating pad. Ice it immediately for 20 minutes after playing. Take aspirin. Do arm-strengthening exercises. A special elbow band that spreads out the muscle pull may provide some relief.

Pulled muscles

Muscles that are subjected to new and different or additional uses are susceptible to muscle fatigue, strains, tears, or cramping—all of which can be avoided 99 percent of the time by proper warm-up and stretching. Generally, beginning tennis players of any age will experience a certain amount of muscle soreness and stiffness, especially in their playing arm and upper and lower legs. Even after all the years Nick and I have played tennis, if we haven't touched a racket for two weeks, we too will feel some muscle soreness when we start up again. So it is not unusual and can be easily alleviated with hot baths and plenty of stretching before and after play.

A pulled or strained muscle is something different, because the muscle has actually been stretched, usually by a sudden motion, farther than it wants to go, and some fibers may even have been torn. Generally, this can be avoided by careful stretching and warm-up, but occasionally a player will slip or try extra hard for a shot and end up with a muscle pull. When this occurs (and you will know because the pain will be more acute and localized, and probably accompanied by swelling to the area), the RICE treatment of rest, ice, compression, and elevation should be followed immedi-

ately for at least 48 hours. This treatment can then be followed by hot baths or, ideally, whirlpools, and always lots of
gentle stretching.

Muscle cramps and heat-related problems

Muscle cramps most commonly occur in hot weather as a
result of dehydration caused by the loss of fluids and minerals from the body through sweating. Thus, in hot weather
it is very important for children to drink plenty of fluids
(preferably water) before, during, and after they play. Thirst
is not a good indicator of how much water should be drunk,
and a child's thirst will probably be quenched long before his
or her body fluid needs have been met. Sugary beverages
such as soft drinks or Gatorade are not recommended, because their high sugar content prevents rapid absorption of
liquid by the body. They just end up sitting in the stomach
during exercise. The replacement of minerals—primarily
salt, potassium, magnesium, and calcium—can be partially
accomplished by eating such foods as whole grains and
green vegetables, for magnesium; oranges, bananas, raisins,
cantaloupes, for potassium; and skim milk, for calcium. Salt
pills are not an appropriate method of inducing water replacement, for several reasons. As Dr. Robert Nirschl stated
in *World Tennis* Magazine (June 1979), "Serious drawbacks
of salt pills include: 1) high incidence of intestinal upset; 2)
tendency to overdose with resultant abnormally high salt
concentrations relative to fluid levels; 3) difficulty in determining proper dosage relative to fluid replacement; and 4)
inconsistent intestinal absorption."

Besides causing muscle cramps, heat can cause exhaustion, manifested in nausea, light-headedness, chills, rapid
pulse, and cold, clammy skin. Sweating is a body's way of
dissipating heat that has built up as a result of increased
work or exercise. Until the body acclimates (seven to ten
days of exercise in hot, humid weather), salt loss through
sweat can be high. After the body has adjusted to the heat,
salt and mineral loss will be reduced, while fluid loss will
continue. Therefore, until a child is used to extreme heat

and humidity, certain precautions can be taken. The first option, of course, is simply not to play, which is advisable if a child does not feel well in any way or has heart or lung problems. Other than that, matches can be scheduled for the cooler parts of the day, many short breaks can be taken, and practices can be made less intense. A child should also towel off frequently, ideally with a towel dipped in cold water. Hats and light-colored clothing can be worn to reflect heat. For fair-complexioned children, a sunscreen should be applied regularly during the time spent in the sun, to prevent sunburn. Most important, a child should drink water throughout the match or practice session. If these suggestions are followed, the chances of heat illness should be minimal. If heat exhaustion symptoms do appear, place the child in a reclining position in a cool, shady place. Replace fluids immediately, release any constricting clothing, and cool the child (with ice bags, fanning, toweling off, etc.). If the child is slow to respond to these aids or develops chest pain, hot and dry skin, or difficulty in breathing, he should be taken to a hospital immediately.

Backaches

First of all, a sore back is nothing to play around with—literally! A sore back can be a symptom of a serious problem or a passing ache, and in a growing child, the pain should be checked out by a qualified orthopedic doctor. We do not feel we are being alarmist, just conservative, in trying to eliminate the physical risks of sport to children. If a child experiences any pain in the back area, play should be stopped and a physician consulted. In most cases, treatment will involve rest, back stretching and strengthening exercises, heat, and perhaps some medication to relax muscles.

Any number of things can cause back pain: incorrect form, poor flexibility, tension, structural weaknesses, a sudden movement, a misstep, or even a sneeze. Although the cause and prevention of back pain is not fully understood, those old stand-bys of proper stretching and warm-up have been proven to be very helpful. Also, strengthening exercises prescribed by a doctor and done routinely, even after the problem has disappeared, are tremendous preventive aids.

Knee problems

A very common childhood problem of the knee is Osgood-Schlatter's disease, better known as "growing pains." It most often occurs in very active, rapidly growing adolescents. During a child's rapid growth, the area high on the shin bone (just below the knee), where the powerful thigh muscle (quadriceps) attaches, is often weak. When this strong quadriceps muscle pulls against the weakened zone on the shin, pain and inflammation can occur. Generally, this is not a serious condition, although it can be quite painful. Rest from running sports is the cure, but in cases where a child can't be tied down, and doesn't mind the pain, ice should be applied immediately after play. When a child stops growing, all such symptoms will cease.

More serious problems of the knee may involve the ligaments and cartilage within and around the joint. If any swelling is apparent, a medical evaluation is recommended. A swollen knee should not be ignored. These more serious problems seldom occur with children or recreational players, and afflict mainly tennis professionals. Pros are constantly playing when overly fatigued, changing court surfaces, overextending themselves, and playing when injured; therefore, it is logical that the more serious injuries occur with them. If a child takes a fall or wrenches his knee in any way to cause pain, rest and ice should be the first treatments. If there is any swelling, or if pain persists for over two days, consult a doctor.

There are also certain structural causes of knee pain. Short, tight calf and hamstring muscles, or weak quadricep muscles (which help support the knee) can contribute to knee problems. Again, stretching and strengthening exercises are the answer. The manner in which weight is distributed on the feet can not only affect the knee but also the foot, ankle, leg, and even back. If a child has a short big toe and a long second toe (Morton's foot), weak arches, or an unstable heel, he may be prone to knee injuries. These problems can be alleviated or averted by seeing a podiatrist, experienced in dealing with runners and athletes, who will probably make shoe inserts (orthotics) for the child. The orthotics will help redistribute the child's weight so that his body will be in better alignment from the feet on up. Orthotics worn in my tennis and running shoes have helped me remedy shin splints, a heel spur, and strained Achilles' tendons, so I can heartily attest to the benefits of my podiatrist, Dr. Murray Weisenfeld in New York, and the orthotics he made for me.

Achilles' tendon strain

The Achilles' tendon runs down the back of the ankle and connects the calf muscle to the heel. It is an appropriately named tendon, because it's a particularly vulnerable spot for injuries. Tennis is a game of footwork, being on the balls of one's feet, changing directions, jumping, and breaking into sudden bursts of speed—all of which put strain on the Achilles' tendon. Besides these possible causes of strain, poorly fitting shoes and tight calf muscles can also be reasons for Achilles' problems. As you can probably guess, stretching and warming up one's body before making any strenuous movements is highly recommended.

If pain and inflammation occur, rest, ice, and very gentle stretching should be the treatment. This is definitely not an injury to fool around with, since it is not uncommon (especially among older athletes) for the Achilles' to snap completely, necessitating surgery and a lengthy recovery program. If the strain is minor, Dr. Weisenfeld recommends putting from one to four spongy powder-puff pads (purchased at any five-and-dime or similar store) into the heel of all the child's flat shoes, especially the tennis shoes. An equal number of sponges should be put in both shoes, so that leg lengths aren't different. These pads serve to cushion and raise the heel, taking pressure off the Achilles' tendon.

Colds and flus

Should a child play if he is not feeling well because of a cold or flu? We suggest not. First of all, no recreational or tournament game is important enough to jeopardize a child's health. Play it safe and wait for the child to recover fully before he goes back on the tennis court. If he is getting cabin fever, explain that practicing in a weakened or irritable state can lead to sloppy habits and sometimes a relapse. After a child is well on the way to recovery, he should take about a week to build up to a normal practice schedule.

Menstrual cramps

Attitudes concerning menstrual cramps have changed quite a bit over the past few years. Years ago, grandmother would take to her bed with aspirin and a hot water bottle at the first sign of a cramp. Today, more and more young girls and women have come to realize that being active does not make cramping any worse and can often help relieve it. Our advice for those girls who experience cramps (there are many who don't at all) is to ignore them as much as possible and carry on as usual. A young woman may be a little more gentle and less demanding with herself because her body may be in a slightly weakened condition, but parents shouldn't let her talk herself into being an invalid either.

WE HAVE COVERED only some of the health problems that we think are pretty common, hoping that a cursory knowledge of them would help parents care for their children. Our advice is hopefully pragmatic, but definitely lay advice. If there are any doubts about an injury or the health of a child, a doctor should be consulted immediately. The area of sports medicine has developed in the past few years, and diagnoses are much more accurate and treatments more effective. Always be on the safe side and seek the help of an expert sports physician.

4.

Physical Conditioning and Nutrition

The Merits of Physical Conditioning

Physical conditioning for the young player serves many purposes, physical and mental. It can make the athlete less vulnerable to injuries, can be the determining factor in the outcome of a competition, and can mentally toughen the athlete by eliminating the fear that he will not be able to "go the distance." Conditioning can also give the player a sense of security during a game—he has fully prepared physically and can now just concentrate on the sport. In addition, there is a circular motivational aspect to conditioning. A child must first be motivated to exercise, but then, because of the time and effort expended, he will be anxious to test its effects on the court. Because beneficial effects will be experienced on the court, the child will then be further motivated to continue conditioning.

Types of Conditioning

In physical training there are two basic areas of focus: exercises to improve cardiovascular efficiency (endurance), and exercises to improve the strength, tone, and flexibility of muscles, ligaments, and tendons. Cardiovascular activity refers to the efficiency of the heart and lungs in processing oxygen and blood through the body. An efficient, healthy heart can pump blood with less effort, has more time to rest between beats, enables a person to exercise longer without getting tired, and responds to physical and emotional crises without racing or making blood pressure rise. Muscular

47

training involves repetitive exercises, usually with weights, in order to strengthen the muscle, which will help prevent injury to the muscle itself and contiguous tendons, ligaments, and joints. Stretching exercises to increase flexibility are also an important part of muscular training.

Cardiovascular Training

In order to build cardiovascular capacity, the President's Council on Physical Fitness recommends at least a half hour per day of exercise to produce any trace of physical fitness. During this half hour, the heart should be functioning at 70 to 80 percent of its capacity. A rough estimate of maximum heartbeat capacity is found by subtracting the person's age from 220. For example, if a child is ten, his estimated maximum heart rate would be 220 minus 10, or 210 beats per minute. For exercise to benefit the heart, the heart rate should be kept between 70 to 80 percent of 210, or between 147 and 168 beats per minute, for at least half an hour.

Fortunately, children seem to have naturally efficient cardiovascular systems. Recent medical research indicates that even "untrained" children have high rates of oxygen intake, which is considered a good measure of heart-lung efficiency. Glover and Shepherd point out in their *Runner's Handbook* that "many nine- and ten-year-old children score higher [on oxygen intake] than all the highly trained distance runners. Most interesting is the fact that the untrained children scored as high as the trained children, which may indicate that endurance is something we are blessed with as children, but squander as we age."

In light of this evidence and the fact that we believe tennis itself is good exercise, we do not see the necessity of extra cardiovascular training for children. By extra training we mean supplemental endurance exercises like running, jumping rope, or cycling. These exercises are not to be discouraged if a child wants to do them, but they certainly are not necessary for the average player. On the other hand, if a child has high competitive goals, stamina will play a major role in his career. Not only should the player be strong enough to endure a long match in the heat of the day, but he should be able to recuperate quickly enough to play several matches a day for a number of consecutive days. No general formula can be given for this type of training, because it must be structured according to the individual's needs, strengths, and weaknesses. Not only are the individual's strengths and weaknesses important, but also his style of play. For instance, Chris Evert's style of play is centered around back-court ball control, and because she does it so well she usually has her opponent on the run, while she stays in one area on the baseline. But Evonne Goolagong Cawley relies heavily on her speed and quickness. Although she has excellent ball control, she astounds her opponents and throws them off-balance by reaching and retrieving hard shots. It follows, therefore, that Evonne's style of play will demand a higher level of fitness than Chris's style. A knowledgeable coach, familiar with a child's goals and needs, would be the best person to design a more rigorous training program for a child.

Muscular Training

Weight lifting is the most common form of muscular training today. More and more professional athletes of both sexes are turning to weight lifting as a supplemental exercise to give them the edge in their sport. Another popular use of weight lifting is in the rehabilitation of injuries. Athletes, both amateurs and pros, are finding that recovery from an injury can be made more quickly and completely with the help of weights. Weight lifting as a sport has also become more popular with both men and women. Men enjoy becoming stronger, building muscle, and giving definition to their bodies. Women, realizing that building bulky muscles could not happen to them the same way it happens to men, because of their different hormonal make-up, find that they can decrease their size and give their bodies better form by toning their muscles and eliminating fat. Weight lifting has even gained in popularity with young athletes, who have turned to it to gain an advantage in various sports and to help them stay in shape during the off-season.

For the young recreational tennis player we do not feel that weight lifting has to be a necessary part of their program. However, if there is a glaring physical weakness or injury that prevents the player from improving, a certain amount of weight lifting is highly recommended. For example, if a boy is constantly twisting or going over on his ankles, he should do some exercises to strengthen the muscles supporting his ankles. To continue to play tennis and hope the problem will disappear is only inviting further injuries. If a young girl is always complaining of a sore playing arm, she probably should do some extra exercises to strengthen it. Just squeezing a tennis ball twenty times a day will help, and probably allow her to play without pain. Getting a child to do these exercises faithfully will probably be a tricky matter. Parents should emphasize that the exercises take only a few minutes a day and that if the child is consistent he can eliminate the physical problem within a few weeks. Even with highly motivated tournament players, it is sometimes difficult to convince them to do weight exercises for their own good. Nick recalls:

I have a young fifteen-year-old girl student who is a very good tournament player, but she could have been great. At thirteen she was ranked number one in the U.S. and Florida for her age division and looked unstoppable. However, she developed a shoulder injury that rest alone would not cure completely, because it left the shoulder weak. What she needed to do was lift weights to get the shoulder strong, even stronger than before, so she wouldn't injure it again. Well, she wouldn't do it, because she was afraid of getting muscular! She was a skinny little thing anyway, but we just couldn't convince her that women can't develop bulky muscles. So she would rest her shoulder and then play until it hurt so much she'd have to rest it again, and so on. Well, it soon affected her mentally and she became afraid to hit certain shots hard, like her serve, because she expected her shoulder to hurt. As a result, her serve never developed into a strong shot and she started losing to people she used to beat.

We're not suggesting that this student should have been pushed into weight lifting. Children should be allowed to make their own choices, but they should also be made fully aware of all the ramifications of their choices by their parents and/or coach.

For those young players who are interested in a complete weight-lifting program we recommend the Nautilus Centers, which are franchised across the country. Nautilus equipment is specially designed to isolate muscle groups in order to work them efficiently and at the same time promote flexibility. The equipment is also designed greatly to eliminate the chances of getting injured through improper use. Another advantage is that, because of the efficiency of the equipment, a complete program working every major muscle group in the body takes only 30 minutes and need be done only three times a week. Generally, there is one-to-one supervision, and it is certainly available upon request. Such players as Billie Jean King, Rosie Casals, and Arthur Ashe have used Nautilus extensively for rehabilitation purposes. One cautionary note: Weight training is most often done by athletes to remedy weaknesses, rehabilitate injuries, or act as a temporary substitute if the athlete is unable to play his own sport. Otherwise, there is no better training for tennis than tennis. If weight lifting is done overzealously, unaccompanied by a good deal of stretching, it can actually hinder tennis improvement by decreasing speed and agility. If a weight program is to be started, the athlete should seek the advice of a physical fitness expert who can design a program specifically for a tennis player.

Stretching

Stretching is the most important supplemental exercise players of any age or caliber can do. Its main function is to prevent injuries, but it also gives the player a feeling of relaxation, readiness, and general well-being. Here are some broad rules to follow for stretching.

1. Stretching is *noncompetitive*. Comparisons with another person or even with oneself are unproductive. One's body should be stretched only as far as it wants to go on any particular day, and it will improve at its own rate.
2. Stretching should be done only to the point just before discomfort. Forcing the body beyond this point is not beneficial and can be harmful.
3. Stretching should be done with grace and relaxation; do not be in a hurry. Never bounce or jerk. And remember always to breathe slowly and evenly.
4. Stretching should be done slowly and held for at least 20 seconds at the farthest point of the stretch.
5. Stretching should be done consistently and always before starting to play.

What follows is an outline of what we feel to be a sufficient pre-tennis warm-up program. Whole books have been written on stretching (see Suggestions for Further Reading), but we are presenting just a few exercises covering the major muscles used in tennis.

1. *Stomach warm-up*   Fifty sit-ups, knees bent, hands behind head.
2. *Ankles, Achilles' tendon, groin, and lower back stretch* (See Figure 1.) With your feet shoulder-width apart and pointed at about a 15-degree angle, heels on the ground, bend your knees and squat. If it is awkward, support yourself against a wall with your hands. Hold the stretch for 30 seconds.
3. *Calf stretch*   (See Figure 2.) Lean against a wall or net post with your arms outstretched. Bend one leg and keep the other one straight behind. Slowly move your hips forward until you feel a stretch in your calf on the straight leg. Be sure to keep the heel on the floor. Hold for 20 seconds and alternate legs.
4. *Achilles' tendon stretch*   (See Figure 3.) Assume the same position as in the calf stretch, but slightly bend

Figure 1. Ankles, Achilles' tendon, groin, and lower back stretch.

the back knee, keeping the heel on the ground. Hold for 20 seconds and alternate legs. This gives you a much lower stretch, which is good for maintaining or regaining ankle flexibility.

5. *Calf and Achilles' stretch* An alternate method of stretching your calf and Achilles' tendon is to stand on a ledge or step with only the balls of your feet and toes on the step. The rest of your foot should be in mid-air. Slowly let your weight drop until your heels are below the level of the step and you can feel the stretch. To stretch your Achilles', assume the above position, with your calf stretched, and slightly bend your knees. Hold for 30 seconds.

6. *Hamstring, arm, shoulder, and back stretch* (See Figure 4.) Grasp a support that is at shoulder height. With

53

Figure 2. Calf stretch.

Figure 3. Achilles' tendon stretch.

Figure 4. Hamstring, arm, shoulder, and back stretch.

your hands shoulder-width apart begin to relax, keeping the arms straight and the chest moving downward, the feet directly under the hips and firmly on the ground. Hold for 20 seconds.

7. *Quadriceps (front thigh) stretch*   (See Figure 5.) Holding on to a support for balance, grab one leg by the top of the foot and pull up and back until a stretch is felt in the quadriceps. Keep the other leg straight. Hold for 20 seconds and alternate legs.

8. *Inside thigh stretch*   (See Figure 6.) In a sitting position, spread your legs as far apart as is comfortable. With the legs held straight and the upper body erect, slowly lean forward at the hips until a good even stretch is felt on the inside thighs. Hold for 20 seconds.

9. *Hamstring and back stretch*   (See Figure 7.) Assume the same seated position, legs apart as in the inside thigh stretch. To stretch the left hamstring and right side of the back, slowly bend forward from the hips toward the foot of the left leg. Keep your head forward and back straight. Hold for 20 seconds. Repeat with the opposite leg.

10. *Back stretch*   (See Figure 8.) Lie on your back with both legs straight. Pull your left leg toward your chest, keeping the back of your head on the ground. Hold for 20 seconds. Switch legs and hold for 20 seconds. Then pull both legs up at the same time and hold for 20 seconds.

11. *Back stretch*   (See Figure 9.) Lie on your back and bend one knee. With your opposite hand, pull the bent leg over your other leg. Turn the head to look toward the hand of the arm that is straight. With the other hand on your thigh, control the stretch by pulling the upper leg down. Hold for 20 seconds on each side.

Do not be deceived by the length of time it took to read about and understand these stretching exercises. Doing them is not complicated and will not take a lot of time. In fact, once you know the routine by heart, it should take only 11 minutes without rushing. Of course, the more time spent

Figure 5. Quadriceps stretch.

Figure 6. Inside thigh stretch.

Figure 7. Hamstring and back stretch.

Figure 8. Back stretch.

58

Figure 9. Back stretch.

stretching, the better, and repeating exercises is certainly beneficial. Children should spend that minimum of 11 minutes stretching, which, in the long run, will save them from spending much more time than that on the injury list or in rehabilitation.

Nutrition

Athletes have long known the benefits of proper nutrition. Because they are attuned to their body's needs and capabilities, they have become aware of which foods are beneficial and which detrimental to their energy output. Unfortunately, this awareness comes later in life, after breaking many bad childhood eating habits. The subject of the young athlete's diet is tricky, because what it really comes down to is the parents' diet. What foods the parents choose to cook and buy are generally what the child eats. Too often parents pass along their bad dietary habits to their children. Foods that are easy or quick are fed to families without thought of the long-term liabilities. Young players do not need anything more than a nutritious and balanced diet, but parents must make this diet available and should serve as proper role models for their children. Many books have been written on this complex subject (see Suggestions for Further Reading), but in this section we are just going to outline what we feel strongly are the necessary basics for a child's nutrition.

The Balanced Diet

There are three basic categories of foods: carbohydrates, fats, and proteins, all of which are necessary for the growth and maintenance of the human body. Balance is achieved when your body is given an ample supply of the necessary vitamins, minerals, amino acids, dietary fiber, and energy through the intake of those three food types. A drastic change in the concept of balance has occurred in the past few years, especially among athletes. The role of proteins has taken a back seat to carbohydrates. A common belief among Americans is that protein is the most essential food, especially for children and athletes, with carbohydrates and fats filling in the gaps. What few people realize is how much fat is hidden in many proteins, so that in reality the average American diet consists of about 40 to 45 percent of total calories in fats, 15 to 20 percent in proteins, and 40 to 45 percent in carbohydrates (mostly refined). The Food and Nutrition Board of the National Research Council, the agency that gives the official recommendations (RDA: Recommended Daily Allowance) for the nutrient requirements in the United States, advises that for a balanced diet a minimum of 20 percent of the daily calories comes from carbohydrates, 10 to 15 percent from proteins, a maximum of 35 percent

Table 1. Recommended and Actual Caloric Intake of Carbohydrates, Proteins, and Fats

	Carbohydrate	Protein	Fat
RDA	20% (minimum)	10–15%	35% (maximum)
Pritikin	80% (unrefined)	10–15%	5–10%
Average American	40–45% (mostly refined)	15–20%	40–45%

from fats, and the remainder from additional carbohydrates and/or proteins. A newer line of thinking (and to our mind better), espoused by Nathan Pritikin, founder and director of the Longevity Center and Longevity Research Institute, recommends that 80 percent of total calories be carbohydrates (mostly complex and unrefined), 10 to 15 percent be proteins, and 5 to 10 percent fats (see Table 1).

Carbohydrates

Carbohydrates consist of simple sugars (glucose, fructose, and so on) or more complex molecules—starches—made up of the simple sugar units. Foods are not exclusively carbohydrates, proteins, or fats but a combination of the three. Examples of foods that are primarily carbohydrate are potatoes, cereals, breads, fruits, and vegetables. The primary role of sugars and starches is to supply energy. (If your body is a fire, carbohydrates are the kindling, whereas proteins and fats are the large logs.) Glucose is the *only* source of food for the brain. Muscles prefer carbohydrates during strenuous exercuse because of carbohydrates' efficient metabolism. Carbohydrates travel through the stomach and intestines quickly, compared with proteins and fats, making them easier to digest while exercising. Also, when broken down through digestion, carbohydrates release a significant amount of water, making them particularly desirable for the athlete in hot weather. Thus, nowadays, it is much more common and healthy to see an athlete having pancakes or a bowl of pasta four hours before his competition than the old-fashioned traditional steak and eggs. The average metabolic transit time for carbohydrates is four hours, as compared with nine hours for proteins and fats. Thus, the pasta eaten four hours before a game will be a source of energy for the competition. On the other hand, the steak will not only be unready to be used for energy but will be extra weight to carry around in the digestive tract during the competition.

As big an advocate of carbohydrates as Pritikin is, he is quick to point out that not all carbohydrates are good. The "bad" carbohydrates, like candy, sugary breads and cereals, and candied fruit he feels are significant causes of ill health. On the other hand, he flatly states that complex carbohydrates like grains, vegetables, and fruits (i.e., minimally refined and processed carbohydrates) are the best foods you can eat. Pritikin feels that besides supplying ample vitamins, minerals, fiber, and energy, their biggest advantage is that they do you no harm. He is talking about the foods that are closest to their natural form: brown rice rather than white rice, whole-wheat flour rather than processed white flour, and fresh fruits and vegetables rather than ones soaked in sugar or preservatives. Be choosy about your carbohydrates, since there is a huge difference between good ones and bad ones. One is life supporting, the other life weakening.

Protein

Proteins are more complex compounds than carbohydrates. Molecularly, they contain carbon, hydrogen, oxygen, and nitrogen, whereas carbohydrates only contain carbon, hydrogen, and oxygen. Protein has many functions in the human body: to build new tissue and repair old tissue; as regulatory substances in salt and water balance; as precursors to hormones, vitamins, antibodies, and enzymes, and as a supplier of energy. Such foods as milk, fish, meat, beans, and eggs are high in protein.

Proteins are composed of amino acids, some of which (nonessential) can be synthesized by the body and some of which (essential) can only be obtained through food. For this reason proteins differ in quality—the greater number of essential amino acids a protein contains, the greater value it is to the human body. However, the foods that are highest in essential amino acids are not necessarily the most healthful, because of their accompanying high levels of fat and cholesterol. According to Pritikin, the use of the common sources of protein (meat, whole milk, eggs) should be reduced because the body's needs for protein have been grossly exaggerated, and because *all* natural food grown contains *all* of the amino acids, essential and nonessential.

Pritikin goes on to say:

> If you think that you'll lack strength and endurance on a diet with 10 percent protein, consider the diet of the Mexican Tarahumara Indians. This diet is roughly the equivalent of the Pritikin Diet (10 percent protein, 10 percent fat, 80 percent complex carbohydrates). On this diet, the Tarahumaras can and do:

• Perform a 500-mile round-trip run in five days.
• Carry a 100-pound pack for 110 miles in seventy hours.
• In their national kickball game, run continuously for forty-eight hours and cover 175 miles. Playing this game, the Tarahumara Indian *women* are known to run continuously for fifty miles at a time!

> These Indians eat animal protein about a dozen times a year. Their diet comprises mainly corn, peas, beans, squash, and other native plants and fruits.
>
> Physicians who have examined these people find them free of cardiovascular disease, hypertension, diabetes, and obesity!

It is worth noting that not a single experiment (and dozens have been performed to test this hypothesis) has demonstrated the benefit of a high protein diet, either for developing muscle strength or endurance.

Fats

Fats, like carbohydrates, contain carbon, hydrogen, and oxygen, but in a different ratio. Fats come in obvious forms like butter, oils, margarine, and lard, but also in less obvious forms like meats, dairy products, seeds, nuts, and eggs. Fats are not inherently harmful, but have very necessary functions. They play an essential role in cellular membrane structure and in hormone synthesis, as well as carrying fat-soluble vitamins like A, D, E, and K.

Fats themselves are not harmful, but their overconsumption can be extremely detrimental to health, and sometimes fatal. Such serious conditions as heart disease and obesity are highly linked with fat. Pritikin finds excess fats cause three kinds of damage.

> First of all, they suffocate your tissues by depriving them of oxygen. Second, they raise the level of cholesterol and uric acid in your tissues, contributing to atherosclerosis and gout. Third, they impede carbohydrate metabolism and foster diabetes.

Americans, with an average intake of fat being 40 and 45 percent of their total calories, certainly do not have to fear a health danger from ingesting too little fat; quite the opposite. Pritikin recommends 5 to 10 percent fat, and the most "fat-free" diets in this country rarely go below 5 percent. Even the poorest Asiatic diet is 10 percent fat. Thus, the main emphasis on the American diet should be to cut back severely on fat ingestion.

Basic Eating Principles

To give you an idea of what a balanced diet would consist of, we again refer to Pritikin.

> To get all the essential vitamins, minerals, and roughage you require, as well as the correct amount of amino acids, you should follow these basic principles:

• *Eat two kinds of whole grains,* such as wheat, oats, barley, brown rice, or buckwheat, every day.

• *Eat some raw vegetable salad and some raw or cooked green or yellow vegetables every day.* Potatoes may be eaten daily if desired.

• *Eat a piece of citrus fruit and up to three additional pieces of fresh fruit daily.*

• *Add beans or peas three times a week* if you like them. Once a week will do if you don't.

• *Eat sweet potatoes or hard yellow squash once or twice a week* if you like them.

• To provide needed vitamin B$_{12,}$ *eat six ounces of low-fat, low-cholesterol animal protein per week*—but not more than one and one-half pounds.

• *Add some unprocessed wheat bran flakes to your diet* (starting with one or two tablespoons a day) *if your bowel elimination is not yet normal.* Otherwise, the diet itself provides all the fiber you need.

• *Eat three full meals daily.* Don't go hungry between meals; eat snacks of whole-grain bread or crackers (ones that are free of oil, fats, added wheat germ, or sugar, honey, or other sweeteners), your fruit allotment, or some raw salad vegetables.

• *Maintain your ideal weight.* This you can do merely by using more or less of the permissible foods according to their caloric values. To lose weight, emphasize the low-calorie raw and cooked vegetables . . . deemphasize the higher calorie foods, e.g., grains, grain products, and beans. To gain weight, do the reverse.

Sugar

Because certain myths exist concerning sugar and athletics, and because of its high consumption among Americans, particularly youngsters, we decided to devote a complete section to it. When we refer to sugar, we're not referring to sugar found in its natural form, such as in an orange or sugar beet, but to sugar in its refined or processed state, such as in a soft drink or candy bar.

Sugar (white, brown, and turbinado), molasses, syrup, and honey are simple carbohydrates that require no digestion and are therefore quickly absorbed into the bloodstream and give a person a quick shot of energy. It is this "quick energy" quality that has given sugar its deceptively good name in athletics. What few people realize is that this quick shot of energy is soon followed by a quick crash or decrease in energy. As sugar is absorbed by the system and released into the bloodstream, the pancreas secretes insulin to bring down the level of blood sugar. The pancreas always releases more than enough insulin to take care of the blood sugar, but the more blood sugar, the more the pancreas "overshoots" its target. Thus, the greater the sugar "high," the greater the subsequent fall. It is this resulting crash that then lures people to eat more sugar to get rid of that down feeling. Have you ever experienced a rumbly stomach and hunger pangs the morning after a huge dinner? This happens because your insulin has shot up so high to compensate for all the blood sugar in your system that it has greatly overshot the target level and brought your blood sugar level crashing down the next morning, leaving you with a feeling of hunger.

More complex carbohydrates, like fruit and natural starches, take longer to metabolize and release sugar (glucose) into the bloodstream slowly and constantly. Thus, the body doesn't go through wild high–low energy cycles, but maintains a rather steady, constant level of energy. This is ideal for athletes and nonathletes alike. Tennis matches are not won by candy bars but by long-term proper diet, training, and preparation.

Besides causing wild, erratic energy swings, refined sugars are totally devoid of nutritional value, but worse, they are vitamin "thieves" because they require vitamins (particularly B vitamins) to be digested. In addition, these sugars also interfere with enzyme activities central to the production of energy. Thus, it's obvious that refined sugar is not healthy for anyone, particularly growing children and growing athletes. The practice by some athletes of popping concentrated refined sugars (dextrose, soft drinks, honey, candy bars) in the heat of competition is not only unhealthy but invites erratic performances. Also, because during physical exercise blood is channeled away from the stomach and to the muscles being used, sugary substances eaten or drunk during a game will probably just sit in the stomach and not pass into the bloodstream. This also applies to the so-called "sweat replacement" drinks like Gatorade, which are far too sugary to be beneficial. Besides, a half-and-half mixture of tomato juice and water is less than 3 percent sugar, therefore is readily absorbed into the bloodstream, and has ample amounts of salt and potassium to replace what was lost in sweating.

Salt

Another myth in sports is that athletes need extra salt to replace what they lose in sweat. As mentioned in the previous chapter, athletes lose not only salt in sweat but magnesium, potassium, and calcium, all of which are necessary minerals and help maintain the body's water balance. Consuming excess amounts of salt therefore does not solve the dehydration problem, but may add to the problem by disturbing the delicate equilibrium among the minerals. Moreover, in adults salt can cause edema (swelling and bloating) and contribute to hypertension.

Salt is not all bad; your body needs some salt. However, the amount needed by most people is amply supplied naturally in almost all foods, so there is no such thing as a totally salt-free diet. We recommend that salt be eliminated entirely from the dining room table, and severely reduced or eliminated from the cooking pot. Changing the salt habit may not be easy the first week, but by the second salt won't be missed, and a heightened taste sensitivity to foods will be noticed.

Preservatives

Various preservatives in commercially packaged, canned and frozen foods have been linked to such things as hyperactivity in children and even cancer. The jury is out on many of those chemicals, and absolute cause-and-effect relations have not yet been firmly established. But why take any chances with a child's health? Try to keep on hand only fresh, preservative-free foods, and be safe. If you aren't in the habit already, start reading the labels of the foods you pick up in the supermarket. Not only will you notice many unpronounceable chemical names, but you will also find many of the sugars and fats hidden in our foods. Some of the sugars will be disguised by the use of their more esoteric names, like sucrose and fructose (any word ending in *-ose* is a sugar), but don't let that fool you, and put those products right back on the shelf. Even most containers of plain table salt are not pure salt but have dextrose added.

Some Helpful Hints

As a stepmother of five children, I'm quite familiar with the intricacies of trying to please everybody. What I've discovered is that it's impossible to please everyone's palates all the time, and democracy in the kitchen doesn't pay. I've found that being autocratic is not only easier for me, but much more helpful for everyone. Here are some helpful pointers.

1. Clean out your kitchen of all junk foods. Read labels and get rid of all the foods with chemical preservatives, sugars, and fats.
2. Keep fresh fruits and vegetables, cut and cleaned, in the refrigerator for snacks. Also, for snacking and to satisfy your child's sweet tooth, keep a plentiful supply of dried fruits like raisins and apricots around.

3. Don't put salt and butter on the table. If your child wants them, let him get up and get them. This is usually a pretty good deterrent.
4. Don't talk about children's diets or how you would like them to eat. Just quietly prepare the meals you think are nutritious and serve them. Children may balk and refuse to eat some things, but eventually their hunger will make them come around. After all, they have no choice.
5. Don't debate or argue. This lets your child know that the issue is closed and saves you a lot of hassle. You wouldn't debate with your child whether or not he should get a polio vaccination, would you?
6. Don't give in. There may be some inconvenience to you and some complaining from your child, but the long-term goals are worth it.

AS A YOUNG TENNIS PLAYER, a child does not have to adopt any supplemental physical fitness routine unless he has a particular weakness or injury to overcome. Of course, proper extra conditioning can be beneficial and should not be discouraged. What we do strongly recommend is a consistent stretching routine to promote flexibility and, most important, to prevent injuries.

There is no special diet for the young athlete other than one that is generally healthful and nutritious for all children. We have no secret dietary concoctions to give a child that winning burst of speed or energy, but what we do offer is the basics of a lifetime eating plan. There is no crash course in physical health or nutrition. There is no substitute for careful preparation, exercise, and good eating habits—the rewards for which can be felt both on and off the court.

5.

The Equipment a Child Needs

Tennis need not be a rich man's sport. Yes, it's true that you can buy rackets that cost over $300, shoes for over $50, strings for $30, and snappy warm-up suits for $100, but these are not necessarily the best for a child, physically or psychologically, even if parents can afford it. In fact, some very high-priced rackets may be just "too much racket" for a child to handle and may actually hinder his improvement. Moreover, for all equipment, the medium-price range provides excellent quality for children, and even for most pros.

Outfitting a child with the high-priced gear can also be psychologically damaging. It can deprive him of self-attained reward and create a false self-image. Pity the poor boy who can't hit a lick who goes out on the tennis court looking like Bjorn Borg. First of all, he may experience some painful peer pressure and ridicule. Other kids may expect him to play better than he does and make fun of him for not being more adept. Second, he might not appreciate the equipment and may develop an attitude of always expecting the best.

Parents shouldn't fool themselves into thinking they're doing their child a favor by buying the "best" and thereby giving him an edge in the game. What a parent may be doing instead is robbing the child of incentives and a sense of accomplishment. It's no accident that many extremely successful people in life have rags to riches backgrounds. Lacking sufficient funds, equipment, and so on, they were forced to plan carefully for specific attainable goals, strive for them, and reap the rewards when they were reached. Setting goals creates incentives, and reaching them gives one a sense of accomplishment, success, and self-worth.

We think having a child *earn* better equipment is a healthy incentive in tennis. A child can learn that through hard work and dedication, he can earn better or newer equipment. When things are obtained in this manner, a child will learn to appreciate and care for them much more, as well as experience a feeling of success in attaining them.

Last, and most important, the "miniature Borg" may feel that his level of play should be as good as his equipment. If he looks like Borg, why shouldn't he play like him, too? He is being set up for failure. The parent has created an ideal self-image that is different from reality. A son knows that he can't play like Borg right now, so why make him feel he is expected to? Let a child use equipment that is comfortable and commensurate with his skills, and eliminate the possibility of creating undue parental pressure.

Another false impression that the "best" equipment can give is to fool a child into thinking it will make him a better player. Fancy rackets don't hit forehands—*players* do, and unless the child understands that there are no easy substitutes for practice, he will not make a great deal of progress.

Rackets

Materials

The number of tennis rackets on the market today is mind-boggling. They come in different weights, sizes, shapes, and materials—all with various advantages and disadvantages. The basic materials that rackets are made of are wood, metal (usually aluminum), fiberglass, graphite, or combinations of these. Until a child develops into an intermediate player with a certain amount of finesse, the standard wood racket will be more than adequate. Besides, despite all the fancy rackets available, more than half the pros still play with wood. So, to start out with, a nice medium-priced (about $35 unstrung) wood racket by any of the major manufacturers (Bancroft, Head, Wilson, Spaulding, Dunlop, etc.) will be of excellent quality. The cheaper rackets will have a tendency to crack or chip. The qualities that a good wood frame offers a player are control, feel, resiliency, and fairly good endurance. Although rackets of other materials can be found in this price range, they may not be of good quality. Also, although those other rackets offer increased power, they sacrifice some control and feel, two qualities we think should be stressed in the early stages of anyone's tennis career. As a player advances in ability, there are some definite advantages of these other materials over wood for certain players. Rackets made by such companies as Head, Prince, PDP, and Yonex offer excellent alternatives to wood.

The most important factors in choosing a racket are that the weight of the racket and size of the grip be comfortable. Rackets come in three weight categories—light, medium, and heavy, representing ranges of weights, not specific weights. Thus, four "light" rackets may each have a slightly different weight. A light racket will be appropriate for most young children, male or female. Of course, the younger and smaller the child, the lighter the racket should be. Some teen-agers may be strong and big enough to handle a medium weight, but this is rare. On the pro tour, most women play with light rackets and most men play with medium. The weight of the racket for your child is important, because a racket that is too heavy can cause fatigue and quite a bit of arm, shoulder, and hand soreness—all of which can take the fun out of tennis.

The proper grip size is important in order to avoid hand and arm soreness and blisters, as well as to give a child a good solid hold on the racket. The grip handles of rackets come in five sizes: 4⅜, 4½, 4⅝, 4¾, and 4⅞ inches in circumference. However, on wood rackets the grips can be filed down or built up to any size; rackets of other materials can only have their grips built up. Most young players will need a 4⅜- or 4½-inch grip. However, there is a precise method of determining the right grip size for any child.

On the palm of the hand there are lateral creases. The

bottom crease, running approximately across the middle of the hand, is the one used for measuring grip size. Take a ruler and measure from the tip of the ring finger (the one next to the pinky) to a point on the crease between the ring and middle fingers. This length corresponds to the correct grip size.

The shapes of grips range from almost square to almost round. Choosing a grip shape is a matter of what feels comfortable, because shapes are all equally good. However, a very round grip is not recommended, because it makes it difficult for the hand to sense exactly where it is on the grip.

Once you have the right weight and grip, the balance of the racket is the next significant factor. A racket's weight can be distributed more toward the head or more toward the handle. An evenly balanced racket will be good for a child. Most rackets are 27 inches long, and if you balance it on your finger 13½ inches up from the handle, it should be balanced, if the weight is evenly distributed.

String

String comes in two kinds of materials, lamb gut and synthetics, which are mostly nylon. Gut ($20 to $30) is by far the best string, giving the most resiliency and feel, luxuries that are wasted on the beginning and intermediate player. Nylon ($10 to $20) on the other hand, though less sensitive, offers greater durability and resistance to humidity and is thus our choice for a child, unless he is an advanced player. Strings also come in different thicknesses or gauges. The higher the gauge number, the thinner the string, and the more sensitive and resilient but the less durable. A medium-gauge string (#15) is sufficient for a child.

The next matter to consider is the tension at which the strings are to be strung. Again, a middle-of-the-road approach is best. Fortunately, racket manufacturers supply recommended string tension and pattern of stringing for each of their racket styles. Make sure the stringer knows and follows these recommendations. To find an expert stringer, ask a club pro or a very good tennis player to suggest someone. Even with the best equipment in the world, if your racket isn't strung properly, it's useless. Once a racket is strung to a child's liking, make a note of the tension (given in pounds) and the type and brand of string used.

Racket and String Care

There are a few things a child can do to help prolong the life of the racket and string. All rackets are sold with covers that should be kept on whenever the racket is not in use. A wood racket should be kept in a press at home to prevent warping. Because rackets get scraped a lot on courts, a strip of adhesive tape on the top of a wood racket will help prevent its wearing down to the strings. Rackets should be kept out of extreme heat or cold, which can warp the frame and cause strings to break. Keeping a racket in a car in the heat of summer or the cold of winter should be avoided. Also, checking a racket with luggage on a plane trip is unwise, since baggage compartments can get very cold. A trick to help preserve gut string is to paint a thin coat of shellac on regularly. This helps delay superficial wear and tear and damage from humidity.

Shoes

Unfortunately, unless a person suffers from a foot ailment, not too much attention is paid to shoes. Children seem to be able to run in anything, so why not keep expenses down and get an inexpensive pair of tennis shoes, since they're going to wear out quickly anyway? Wrong! Here is one area where parents should make the commitment to spend whatever money it takes to get an excellent fit for their child. A good shoe is not only important for a child's comfort and effectiveness on the court, but also for his growth and bone development. Improper shoes on children or adults can lead to many problems, from blackened toenails and blisters to Achilles' tendinitis and heel spurs. To avoid these problems, the first consideration should be to purchase a shoe made specifically for tennis, and not for track or boating. There are many excellent shoes on the market today, but there are also some lemons. Learn what to look for in a good tennis shoe and a wise purchase will be easy.

The most noticeable aspect of a shoe is its comfort and how it fits the child's foot. Be warned, though, that comfort doesn't necessarily equal quality. There are a number of shoes (like Tretorn) on the market that are exquisitely comfortable but offer little support or durability. A shoe should be snug but not tight, leaving about one-half inch between the tip of the longest toe and the end of the shoe. The heel should be held firmly by the shoe to avoid chafing and blisters. Some styles of shoes are made narrower than others, so be sure to try out a few different styles. If greater width is desired, women should try the men's styles or sizes. I like shoes with lace-to-toe lacing (having at least six eyelets rather than four), because I can adjust the snugness of the shoe myself through the tightness of the lacing at various points. Make sure tennis socks are used during the fitting in order to get an accurate size.

The tops of tennis shoes are made of either canvas or leather. Canvas is lighter and allows the foot to "breathe" more, since it is a more porous material than leather. It is also less expensive, running between $20 and $30. Leather, on the other hand, though more costly ($30 to $35), offers firmer support for the foot and ankle and greater durability.

Support

The things I look at for support in a tennis shoe are the arch, heel counter, raised heel, and sole thickness. Most tennis shoes come with an arch support, but make sure that the construction fits the child's particular arch. If it does, it should hardly be noticeable.

A high heel counter is desirable because it helps support the ankle and helps prevent the foot from turning over on its side. This is important, because in tennis one is constantly moving laterally and changing directions, and firm support

Heel
Counter

Higher
Heel

◄— Sole

Figure 10.

along the sides of the shoe is necessary to prevent accidents. A high heel counter is also handy in case heel pads ever have to be inserted under the child's heel in the shoe. With a low heel counter a child's foot may be riding too high in the shoe, making it possible for the foot to turn over sideways or come out of the shoe entirely.

A good shoe should have a thick sole that is somewhat higher at the heel. The sole not only serves as padding between the foot and ground but as insulation against the heat and friction from the court. A raised heel relieves strain on the Achilles' tendon and calf muscle and gives extra protection against bone bruises to the heel. Soles are made either from rubber or polyurethane. Although polyurethane offers greater lightness, rubber is more durable and softer. In most cases the tread on the bottom of the soles will be in either a nubbed or herringbone pattern; both are equally good. Just avoid smooth soles because, like a bald tire, they offer little stopping power.

Care

Regrettably, shoes will wear out and will be, next to tennis balls, the most perishable pieces of equipment a child will need. However, here are some tips to help prolong the life of a child's shoes.

One highlight of canvas shoes is that they can be put in the washing machine. Fine and good, but by all means avoid the dryer. Not only could a size 5 turn into a size 3, but some of the sole may be found dripping from the insides of your dryer. If a child's shoes last long enough to be washed, set them in the sun or a warm place to dry.

Most sports and tennis shops carry a rubber-cementlike substance ("shoe goo") that can be used to repair worn patches on the soles of tennis shoes. Since it is the toes of shoes, rather than the bottoms, that wear out first, application of the "goo" on the toes will slow down wear. However, if this "goo" is placed on the bottoms, it can be dangerously slippery. A better way of coping with worn-out bottoms is to find a shoe or sports store that does resoling for leather shoes. For $15 to $20 an expensive pair of leather shoes can be entirely resoled and will be almost as good as new.

Clothing

Years ago an eleven-year-old Billie Jean King was lining up at the Los Angeles Tennis Club for an official group picture with her peers. Perry T. Jones, the czar of tennis in southern California at that time, asked her to please step out of the picture because she was not "properly dressed." She was wearing shorts. Fortunately, this kind of snobbery and narrow tennis etiquette doesn't exist today, and the spectrum of clothes worn on the court is far greater.

"White is right" used to be the predominant clothes policy in tennis. Today, except for a few "eastern establishment" clubs, anything goes, as long as the clothes are kept clean and fresh. Any color of the rainbow is permissible, but a few considerations for weather conditions should be made. Since dark colors absorb sunlight and heat, on a hot, humid day light-colored or white clothing is much more comfortable. Conversely, on a cold day dark colors will help trap what heat and sunlight there is.

Technically, any pair of comfortable shorts and a T-shirt are enough for a child to start playing tennis. Just because a child wants to try a new sport, a new wardrobe isn't necessary. However, if a child could use more "tennis-y" clothes, here are some suggestions. The important thing is that whatever children wear, they should be comfortable, physically and mentally. Although dresses and skirts are the more common wear among girls at tournaments, shorts are perfectly acceptable (sorry, Perry T.). In fact, on the practice court in parks and clubs, shorts are quite common. For boys, shorts and T-shirts or shirts with collars are standard gear. Shirts and dresses should have ample room in the armholes to allow for a full range of movement. Shorts and skirts should fit at the waist, but without tightness or pinching. Dresses and skirts should be long enough to cover a girl's bottom. Nothing is worse than feeling "exposed" on the court. Light cottons, synthetics, or combinations of the two are good clothing materials. Cottons allow the skin to breathe more, but synthetics dry faster and don't get as heavy with sweat during a game. Whatever you do, get a wash-and-wear material. Tennis clothes are worn and washed a lot, so they can be a real nuisance if they have to be ironed each time.

Other necessary items of clothing are a warm jacket or sweater and a sweatsuit or warm-up suit. A child should be taught the importance of keeping warm at all times. This is particularly true right after a game, when he can then become vulnerable to colds and stiff muscles. Children should be taught to wrap up right away. On cold days a child may even want to play in warm-up pants to keep his legs warm throughout the game.

Lastly, whatever a child wears, it is his choice. With the variety of clothes available today, the temptation is great to dress a son or daughter to look like Jimmy Connors or

Chris Evert, which is fine as long as the child wants it. Remember, when a child walks on the court, he shouldn't be thinking about looking like a tennis player, but about being a player.

Balls

Tennis balls are the most perishable items of equipment a child will need. A good can of three new balls can cost between $2 (at some sports shops) and $4 (at some clubs) but will last only about three playing hours. Brand-new balls are not necessary every time your child goes out to play, but "dead" or "bald" balls should not be used either. A dead ball is one that can be pushed in and indented by the fingers more than ¼ inch, and consequently does not bounce high or come off the racket with much force. A bald ball has lost the outer covering of fuzz, which causes air friction, and flies through the air too quickly. A dead ball is bad to play with, because it takes too much effort to hit it over the net, causing arm fatigue and stress as well as giving a much different feel for the game. A bald ball is very hard to control and gives yet a different feel.

In the United States, most balls sold are pressurized, that is, they are filled with compressed air and sealed in an airtight can for freshness. (When opening a new can of balls, you should always hear air escape; otherwise the balls are dead and should be replaced by the seller.) Unpressurized balls are not filled with compressed air and come in a cardboard box. These balls tend to be much heavier and more durable. Even though these balls maintain their hardness, they can become rocklike and leaden and consequently very hard on the arm. The top brand pressurized balls in the United States are Wilson, Penn, and Bancroft, with Spaulding and Dunlop running a close second.

Used balls in fairly good condition can be purchased at some sports or tennis shops, or in larger quantities from tournaments. These can be a wise buy, especially if a child is still in the "wild" stage and loses balls over the fence.

Courts

If you visit several tennis courts around the world, or even in your own area, you will notice two things. First, the size and the dimensions of the courts will be identical because they are standardized. Second, many courts will have vastly different surfaces. In fact, no two court surfaces will be absolutely alike.

In general, there are five different types of court surfaces: hard court, clay, grass, wood, and carpet. The way the ball reacts to each of these surfaces varies quite a bit and demands different stroke timing and strategies. Even within each category, the surfaces can vary substantially.

Hard courts in the United States (in Great Britain, *hard court* means clay) are made of either cement or asphalt and are considered a fast surface. However, the speed can be greatly altered by making the surface smoother (faster) or rougher (slower). The speed of a court refers to how fast the ball comes off the playing surface. Asphalt courts are a trifle softer than cement and therefore are a bit easier on the legs. Most courts on the West Coast are made of either cement or asphalt.

Clay courts are a soft, slow surface, generally consisting of unmixed clay, a mixture of clay and brick, or stone dust. The surface is rather sandy or "gravelly," which slows the speed of the ball down considerably and forces one to slide while changing directions, stopping, or starting to run for a ball. Because of this different footing and court speed, clay-court strategies are quite different from hard-court strategies. On clay one is more apt to stay back on the baseline and have long backcourt rallies, while on most hard courts a serve-volley game is quite effective. Clay courts have various trade names (Har-Tru, En-Tout-Cas, Rubico, Tenico) and are widely seen in the East, South, and Midwest, as well as most of Europe and South America.

Grass is quickly becoming an extinct surface, because of its fragility and maintenance expense. In appearance it is much like a golf green, only with a much harder under-surface. Because the ball skids as it strikes the grass, the bounce is low and fast. The bounce of the ball can often be maddeningly unpredictable, since grass can never be made absolutely even. Most grass courts are on the East Coast in private clubs and in England and Australia. Wimbledon, the most prestigious tournament in the world, and the Australian championships are still played on grass.

Wood is another rare surface, usually seen as makeshift courts in school gyms or as indoor courts in England. Wood is a lightning-fast surface with an even bounce. Because it is so fast, the ball can be easily put away with a hard shot, consequently making rallies short.

Carpet is a surface that developed with professional tennis. Because the floors on school gyms and arenas were unsatisfactory, the touring pros devised a movable court that traveled with them that could be laid down on almost any surface. Today it is still the predominant surface for the indoor pro circuit and is used in many indoor facilities in the east. The speed is much like hard courts, but because of the thickness of the carpet one's legs do not take the beating they do on cement and asphalt.

IF YOU'RE STARTING from scratch, tennis equipment may sound confusing and expensive, but it is not. The initial outlay for racket, string, and shoes might be around $70, far cheaper than many other sports, such as skiing, hockey, or golf. Since a racket can last for years and there are many free public facilities available, regular expenses will be for just shoes and balls. Fortunately, there is very high quality within a medium cost range in tennis equipment, making it unnecessary to spend a lot of money. However, do spend some time learning about proper equipment, to give your child a good start in the game.

6.

Where a Child Can Play

Depending on where you live, finding a court to play on can be as easy as lacing on your shoes or as difficult as trying to play with an unstrung racket. If you happen to live in southern California, you probably have twenty public courts within a mile of your home. In Hopewell Junction, New York, it might be a totally different story. You might find yourself scrambling over just a few courts, and paying a hefty fee for the right to play on them. Financial considerations cannot be ignored and are often topmost in many parents' minds when trying to decide on a tennis facility. Is it necessary to join a club to find good competition? Do public courts have good coaches? Will a child's tennis suffer because parents can't do more financially? In this chapter we will answer these questions as well as discuss where to find tennis facilities, what they have to offer in terms of organized programs and coaching, and what the approximate costs might be.

Where to Play

If all the tennis pros were polled and asked where they hit the most balls during the first two years of their careers, I bet most would say against a garage door or backboard. In fact, what parents should think of if their child starts tennis is whether or not they can afford a new garage door! A backboard (wall, garage door, or whatever) should never be underrated. Not only is it a beginner's most reliable practice partner, but even some accomplished players use it regularly. In 1975, I was in the ladies' dressing room at Wimbledon having just finished warming up Billie Jean King for her final against Evonne Goolagong for the ladies' championships. For the entire two weeks of the tournament, practice courts had been a real nuisance to reserve—too many players chasing too few courts. The process of hassling for a practice court every day, just to rush through your allotted 30 minutes of practice time, only added to the tension we all already felt from the tournament itself. Standing in the dressing room, it occurred to me that I had hardly seen Evonne during the two weeks, and never on the practice courts. Curious to know how she had handled the practice court problems, I asked her who she had been warming up with all tournament. "Aw, occasionally Roger [Cawley, her husband] and I go to this other club, but mostly I've just been hitting up against the backboard. Don't have to worry 'bout getting bumped off that way." For the finals of the most prestigious tournament in the world, when most players go through elaborate, ritualistic practices, Evonne Goolagong had warmed up against a backboard! I'm not exactly recommending this procedure to tournament players, since Evonne went on to be crunched 6–0, 6–1 by Billie Jean, but this result was due more to Billie Jean's flawless play that day than to any lack of preparation on Evonne's part. After all, her routine did get her through two grueling weeks to the finals.

Never let a child be discouraged if a court or opponent can't be found. Just grab some balls and head for the nearest large vertical surface. Good backboards can be found at most schools and parks and are rarely fully occupied. Also, for players of any level there are numerous drills and games to play against a backboard, some of which will be covered in Chapter 9, on practice.

Schools and Public Parks

The quality of a tennis facility is dependent on a number of criteria. How many courts are available? Are they crowded? Is there a court fee? How much? Is the facility in a good neighborhood? Is there supervision? Are the courts well maintained? Are there locker rooms? Is there a junior program?

How favorably each one of these questions can be answered depends a great deal on where you live. Within a five-minute car ride of where I lived in Santa Monica, there were at least fifty well-kept school or park courts available at no cost. Locker rooms were scarce, but they were unimportant, since the weather was always temperate and I could make it home before getting chilled. In addition, not only was there an excellent junior program run by the city's recreation department, but the Santa Monica Tennis Patrons also sponsored and ran junior activities. Thus, it's easy to see why southern California has been the breeding ground for so many of the world's best players, including Billie Jean King, Stan Smith, Bob Lutz, Tracy Austin, and Karen Hantz Susman. Nowadays, however, "good-weather states" no longer dominate the tennis scene. With the advent of the tennis boom, excellent facilities, public and private, popped up all over the nation, encouraging youngsters to play. As a result, some cold-weather eastern states have produced fine talents, such as John McEnroe, Vitas Gerulaitis, and Pam Shriver. In fact, Vitas, realizing his debt to the public parks system around New York City where he grew up, has formed his own summer junior program in which he and some of his friends, such as Bjorn Borg and Arthur Ashe, give free instructional clinics to youngsters and pass out free rackets, to boot!

The advantages of school and park facilities are that courts are plentiful, nearby, and cost a minimal amount, if anything at all. Also, many fine junior programs are run on these courts by city recreation departments. These programs, or the opportunity to develop them, often attract top-flight coaches. These dedicated people relish the thought of running large public programs where the chance of developing young talent is great. Jimmy Evert, Chris's father, is a perfect example of just such a coach, at Holiday Park Tennis Center in Fort Lauderdale.

A disadvantage of public courts is that they can be crowded, which means waiting for a court and a limited amount of time to play. They can also be noisy because of other nearby activities, such as, perhaps, a Little League game. (This noisiness, however, can become an asset, since it can train a player to block out all distractions and to concentrate only on the game.) Occasionally, these courts are poorly maintained, resulting in torn nets and cracks in the surface. On the whole, though, public park courts, or courts at the local elementary, junior high, or high school, or city or state college offer an accessible and totally adequate place to play tennis, especially for a child in the early stages of involvement with the sport.

In July 1979, *Tennis* Magazine listed their choices of the fifty greatest municipal tennis facilities, based on the number of courts, the court's lighting, its maintenance, reservation system and fees, coaching and junior programs, pro shops and locker rooms, and general ambience. The table that begins on page 104 shows their picks.

The junior programs offered at most municipal facilities offer a minimum amount of instruction during the school year. Generally, youngsters will gather once a week for two hours of hitting the ball and playing against one another, with one or two instructors organizing and supervising the activities. These groups give a child a good chance to practice what he has been taught in private lessons and to meet and make friends with new practice partners. During the summer, more instructors and courts are available, making it possible for more group instruction.

Tennis and Country Clubs

This category of facilities includes both those clubs that require membership fees and those that don't but have substantial court fees ($10 to $18 per hour). Generally, clubs have nicer ambience, better locker rooms, and are maintained better than municipal facilities. However, the caliber of competition, coaching, and junior programs, and availability of courts are not necessarily better. And, of course, the price is much higher than public courts. A reasonably nice tennis club in southern California costs about $4,000 to join, with dues about $40 per month, but no separate court fees. In the east, rates for joining a club are about $500 with no monthly dues, but there is a court fee of around $15 per hour each time you play.

The advantages of a club include friends, a convenient location near your home, a feeling of safety for a child (although this is not necessarily true), and other amenities, such as a pool or snack bar. A disadvantage of clubs may be a lack of variety in competition that public courts have, and a child may become spoiled and pampered. Even now I experience this drawback when I go back to my club in Los Angeles to play. The Riviera Tennis Club is perfect in every way—good competition, beautiful courts, picturesque atmosphere—too perfect. When I play tournaments elsewhere, things seem a great deal less than perfect in comparison. I find I have to concentrate doubly hard not to let little things bother me, things I never run into at the Riviera—a slick court, a torn net, an unattractive background, and so on. In the same way, a child could end up being finicky about where he plays. Children growing up on public courts learn to adapt to many different situations, a habit that eventually increases their powers of concentration.

Junior programs at clubs are quite similar to those at municipal courts, but the types of young players at clubs tend to be different. Generally, children in junior programs at public courts are self-motivated and are there because they want to be. Often at clubs, children are in programs because their parents have chosen that over a babysitter, or the parents are on another court playing and want their child to be occupied. Therefore, the programs at clubs tend to be more socially instead of competitively oriented. These programs do, however, make competition available and are excellent places for your child to make new social contacts.

A typical school-year routine for a club junior program would entail two hours, one day a week with about five to ten children per court. The first hour would be spent warming up, rallying, and practicing the serve. The second hour would consist of a group instructional demonstration by an instructor, matches, and game-type drills. This type of program costs about $40 for ten two-hour sessions. Summer programs are more intense and are geared more to teaching. They may have two two-hour sessions per week for four weeks at a cost of $120 per session.

On page 111 are *Tennis* Magazine's (November 1979) choices for the top fifty indoor and outdoor clubs.

Summer Camps

Another type of facility to consider for children is a summer tennis camp. These camps put a strong emphasis on tennis and therefore should be only for the child who is willing to make a definite commitment to tennis. If all a child wants is a summer-camp experience, then choose one that doesn't revolve around just one sport but offers a variety of activities. For the serious young player, summer camps can be invaluable. By experiencing a heavy tennis schedule, the child can make a more educated decision about being a more serious player. This is not to say that a beginner or less serious player would be totally out of place in a tennis camp. There are plenty of other activities and social functions, and some camps (like Nick's at Wayland Academy in Beaver Dam, Wisconsin) will tailor-make a suitable program for each child, to make sure that camp always remains fun. For example, a beginning player may not spend as much time on the court or in formal instruction, and have more time for other activities and leisure. Here is a sample weekday schedule at Nick's camp:

Sample Daily Schedule at the Nick Bollettieri Tennis Camp

7:00	Wake-up and room cleaning
7:45	Breakfast
8:15–8:45	Semiprivate instruction

8:45–9:00	Warm-up and stretching exercises
9:00–11:30	Stroke drills, agility and footwork drills with 6–8 pupils/court
11:30–12:00	Semiprivate instruction
12:00–12:30	Lunch
12:30–1:30	Semiprivate instruction (2 or 3 students per court with 1 instructor). Each student seen at least once a week
1:30–4:00	From 2 to 6 students on a court playing singles and doubles points. Strategy emphasized.
4:00–5:00	Semiprivate instruction
5:00–6:00	Dinner
6:00–8:30	Singles and doubles play. Lecture on strategy.
8:30–9:45	Free activities: TV, social functions, backgammon, swimming
9:45	Bedtime

Saturdays and Sundays are open days when the students can go shopping, play tennis if they like, or indulge in any of the other camp activities.

There are several elements parents should look for when deciding on a camp for their child. First, make sure there is good supervision on and off the court. The ratio of instructors and counselors to students should help give you an idea about supervision; the lower the ratio, the better the supervision, in most cases. Second, make sure the camp director is in residence. Many camps will advertise a famous camp director who in actuality is too busy playing tournaments ever to run a camp and makes only rare appearances. This kind of camp may still be good, but know what you're getting for your money. Third, make sure the instructors are qualified tennis teachers. You don't want some gym teacher who only plays occasionally as an instructor, or some teen-ager looking for a fun summer. You do want an accomplished player who can teach what he knows. Ask the camp for a summary of the backgrounds of the instructors. Fourth, make sure the facilities are clean and large enough for the number of students. Ideally, in areas where the weather can be extremely hot and humid or rainy, indoor and outdoor courts should be available. However, all camps should have some indoor activity area for games on rainy days. Fifth, make sure other activities like swimming, hiking, riding, and so on are available. Your child won't want to play tennis all the time. Also, if a child is kept busy and has little idle time, he will be less likely to get homesick and will have more fun.

The following is a list of the camps Nick and I feel fulfill the above criteria. There are probably some very good camps we've missed, but these are the ones on which we have first-hand knowledge:

Recommended Tennis Camps for Young Players

California

Allen Fox Malibu Tennis Camp
Pepperdine University, Malibu. Coed (10–18). 17 courts. 6:1 ratio. July–August. $550/2 weeks. Write: Allen Fox, Dept. of Athletics, Pepperdine University, Malibu, Calif. 90265.

Bassett-Martin Tennis Camp
The Cate School, Santa Barbara. Coed (9–18). 8 courts. 5:1 ratio. 2-week sessions. June 29–August 8. Write: Bassett-Martin Tennis Camp, 1 Coral Tree Lane, Rolling Hills Est., Calif. 90274. (213) 377-0086.

Ed Collins USD Tennis School
San Diego. Adults, juniors (10–18). 8 courts. 6:1 ratio. 6-day, 2-week sessions. June–August. $175/6 days (day), $245/6 days (resident). Write: Ed Collins, Tennis Coach, University of San Diego, San Diego, Calif. 92110. (714) 291-6480, ext. 4272.

Dennis Ralston–Charlie Pasarell Tennis Camp
California Lutheran College, Thousand Oaks. Coed (9–18). 10 courts. 6:1 ratio. July–August. $265/week, $510/2 weeks, $745/3 weeks. Write: Sportsworld, 8245 Ronson Road, Suite D, San Diego, Calif. 92111. (714) 279-7800, (800) 542-6005 (Calif. residents).

Dennis Ralston–Charlie Pasarell Tennis Camp
Point Loma College, San Diego. Coed (9–18). 8 courts. 6:1 ratio.
July–August. $265/week, $510/2 weeks, $735/3 weeks. Write:
Sportsworld, 8245 Ronson Road, Suite D, San Diego, Calif. 92111.
(714) 279-7800, (800) 542-6005 (Calif. residents).

Dennis Ralston–Charlie Pasarell Tennis Camp
Sonoma State College, Rohnert Park. Coed (9–18). 12 courts. 6:1
ratio. July–August. $265/week, $510/2 weeks, $735/3 weeks.
Write: Sportsworld, 8245 Ronson Road, Suite D, San Diego, Calif.
92111. (714) 279-7800, (800) 542-6005 (Calif. residents).

John Gardiner's Tennis Ranch
Carmel Valley. 12 courts. 3:1 ratio. Coed (9–16). June 15–August 16. $850/3 weeks. Adults. March 26–June 15, August 17–November 26. $775-$850/week. Write: John Gardiner Tennis Ranch,
Box 228, Carmel Valley, Calif. 93924. (408) 659-2207.

Rancho Bernardo Inn Tennis College
San Diego. Adults, juniors (12 and up). 16 courts. 6:1 ratio. 2-, 3-,
4-, 5-day sessions. All year. Write: Rancho Bernardo Inn Tennis
College, 17550 Bernardo Oaks Drive, San Diego, Calif. 92128.

Tony Trabert Tennis Camp
Thacher School, Ojai. Coed (10–18). 10 courts. 6:1 ratio. June
22–August 23. $800/3 weeks. Write: Tony Trabert Tennis Camp,
1101 So. Robertson Blvd., Los Angeles, Calif. 90035. (213) 274-5383.

Vic Braden Tennis College
Trabuco Canyon. Adults, juniors (9 and up). 16 courts. 6:1 ratio.
Sessions all year. $125/2 days, $200/3 days, $300/5 days. Write: Vic
Braden Tennis College, P.O. Box 438, Trabuco Canyon, Calif.
92678. (714) 581-2990.

Colorado

Cliff Buchholz Tennis Camp
Colorado State University, Fort Collins. Coed (10–18). 13 courts
(5 indoor). 5:1 ratio. June 15–August 9. $260/week. Write: Cliff
Buchholz Tennis Camp, 1800 Heath Pkwy., Fort Collins, Colo.
80524. (303) 493-7305.

Connecticut

All American Sports
Hotchkiss School, Lakeville. Coed (8–18). 36 courts (10 indoor). 5:1 ratio. June 17–August 18. $340/week. Write: All American Sports, 366 Madison Ave., New York, N.Y. 10017. (212) 697-9220.

Ron Holmberg Tennis Camp
Kent School, Kent. 23 courts (4 indoor). 4:1 ratio. Coed (10–16). 1-, 2-, 3-week sessions beginning in June. Adults. Mini-weeks beginning in May. Write: Ron Holmberg Tennis Camps, 31 Roe Ave., Box W-C, Cornwall-on-Hudson, N.Y. 12520. (914) 534-2211.

Welby Van Horn Tennis Camp
The Choate School, Wallingford. 40 courts (13 indoor). 3–4:1 ratio. June–August. Coed (9–18). $295/week. Adults. $225/mini-week, $350/week. Write: Welby Van Horn Tennis Camp, Box 259, Gracie Station, New York, N.Y. 10028. (212) 734-1037.

Florida

Crookenden's Commonsense Camp
Indian Harbor Beach. Coed (10–18). 30 courts. 6:1 ratio. June 15–August 23. $425/2 weeks, $200/additional weeks. Write: Crookenden's Commonsense Camp, The Pines Resort & Tennis Club, 1894 S. Patrick Dr., Indian Harbor Beach, Fla. 32937. (305) 773-2000.

Harry Hopman's International Tennis at Bardmoor
Largo. 42 courts. 4:1 ratio. Coed (9–19). May 25–August 30. $375/week, $750/2 weeks, $365/additional weeks, up to 14 weeks. November–May, $455/week. Adults. All year. $450–$675/5 days. Write: Harry Hopman, Camp Director, 8000 Bardmoor Blvd., Largo, Fla. 33543. (813) 393-5461/5666.

Newk's Junior Tennis Camps in Florida/John Newcombe's Vacation Resort
Clermont. 17 courts. 4–5:1 ratio. Coed (10–18). June–August. $275/week, $550/2 weeks, $825/3 weeks, $1,100/4 weeks. Adults. 3-, 6–day sessions. All year. Write: Barney Barber, Camp Director, Newk's Junior Camps, Rte. 1, Box 25-E3, Clermont, Fla. 32711. (904) 394-6171.

Hawaii

Peter Burwash International Junior Tennis Camp
Oahu. Coed (12–18). 10 courts. 4:1 ratio. July 1–August 7. $1,250/5 weeks. Write: Peter Burwash International, 1909 Ala Wai Blvd., Suite 1507, Honolulu, Hawaii 96815.

Idaho

John Gardiner's Tennis Camp
Sun Valley. Coed (8–17). 6 courts. 3:1 ratio. June 9–August 25. $550/2 weeks, $750/3 weeks. Write: John Gardiner Tennis Ranch, 5700 E. McDonald Dr., Scottsdale, Ariz. 85018. (602) 948-2100.

Illinois

Ramey Tennis Schools
Knox College, Galesburg. 10 courts (3 indoor). 4:1 ratio. Coed (10–18). June 8–July 26. $250/week, $475/2 weeks. Adults. June 29–July 26. $175/weekend, $295/week, $230/week (day). Write: Ramey Tennis Schools, Rte. #6, Owensboro, Ky. 42301. (502) 771-4723/5590.

Maryland

Don Budge Tennis Campus
McDonogh. Coed (10–18). 21 courts. 4:1 ratio. June 15–August 16. $750/3 weeks (resident), $395/3 weeks (day). Write: Don Budge Tennis Campus, 275 Lincoln Ave., Brentwood, N.Y. 11717. (516) 231-7550.

Massachusetts

All American Sports
Deerfield. Coed (8–18). 30 courts (6 indoor). 5:1 ratio. June 24–August 11. $295/week. Write: All American Sports, 366 Madison Ave., New York, N.Y. 10017. (212) 697-9220.

New England Tennis Camp
Lawrence Academy, Groton. Coed (14–16). 24 courts (8 indoor). 5–6:1 ratio. 2-, 4-week sessions. June 23–August 25. Write: Jay Norek, Camp Director, New England Tennis Camp, South Road, Harrison, N.Y. 10528. (914) 835-3030.

Offense-Defense Tennis Camp
Curry College, Milton. Coed (10–18). 39 courts (12 indoor). 4:1 ratio. June 22–August 16. $235/week. Write: Judy and Mike

Meshken, Camp Directors, Offense-Defense Tennis Camp, P.O. Box 295, Trumbull, Conn. 06611. (203) 374-7171.

Michigan

Don Kerbis Tennis Ranch
  Watervliet. 25 courts. 4:1 ratio. Coed (10–18). June 16–August 10. $550/2 weeks. Adults. June–August. $150/weekend, $325/ week. Write: Don Kerbis Tennis Ranch, 9327 Red Arrow Hwy., Watervliet, Mich. 49098. (616) 463-3151.

New Jersey

Alex Mayer's Camp Tennis
  Centenary College, Hackettstown. Coed (9–17). 4:1 ratio. 2-, 4-, 6-, 8-week sessions. June–August. Write: Alex Mayer's Camp Tennis, 1 Brockden Drive, Mendham, N.J. 07945. (201) 543-7227.

Alex Mayer's Camp Tennis
  Craigmeur, Newfoundland. Coed (9–17). 17 courts (9 indoor). 4:1 ratio. Weekly sessions. June–August. Write: Alex Mayer's Camp Tennis, 1 Brockden Drive, Mendham, N.J. 07945. (201) 543-7227.

Charlie Lundgren's Camp Racquet
  Blairstown. Coed (9–17). 20 courts (6 indoor). 4:1 ratio. June 29–August 9. $695/3 weeks, $1,390/6 weeks. Write: Charlie Lundgren, Camp Director, 153 Franklin Street, Bloomfield, N.J. 07003. (201) 743-3607.

Frank Brennan Tennis Academy
  The Peddie School, Hightstown. 19 courts (5 indoor). 5:1 ratio. Coed (8–17). June 22–August 15. $275/week, $525/2 weeks, $950/4 weeks. Adults. June 15–21. $190/3 days, $360/week. Write: Frank X. Brennan, Jr., 695 Panchita Way, Los Altos, Calif. 94022. (415) 948-8781.

New York

New England Tennis Camp
  Pawling. Coed (11–15). 24 courts (12 indoor). 6:1 ratio. 4-week sessions. June 23–August 25. Write: Norman Winik, Camp Director, New England Tennis Camp, South Road, Harrison, N.Y. 10528. (914) 835-3030.

Ohio

Ramey Tennis Schools
Ohio Wesleyan University, Delaware. Coed (14–18). 21 courts (6 indoor). 4:1 ratio. June 15–August 16. $250/week, $475/2 weeks, $175/week (day). Write: Ramey Tennis Schools, Rte. #6, Owensboro, Ky. 42301. (502) 771-4723/5590.

Pennsylvania

Chase Tennis Center
Westtown School, Westtown, Pa. Coed (11–17). 26 courts (6 indoor). 5:1 ratio. June 21–August 20. $875–$925/4 weeks. Write: Neil Chase, Chase Camps, Box 1446 W.T., Manchester, Mass. 01944. (617) 526-7514.

Frank Brennan Summer Tennis School
Mercersburg Academy, Mercersburg, Pa. 20 courts (3 indoor). 3½:1 ratio. Coed (8–18). 2-, 4-, 6-, 8-week sessions. June 15–August 9. $495/2 weeks. Adults. June 8–14. $175/mini-week, $325/week. Write: Frank Brennan, Camp Director, Box 126 W, Ramsey, N.J. 07446. (201) 327-1758/8087.

South Carolina

Clemson Tiger Tennis Camp, Inc.
Clemson University, Clemson. Coed (9–17). 27 courts (2 indoor). 4:1 ratio. June 8–27. $190/6 days. Write: Chuck Kriese, Camp Director, P.O. Box 31, Clemson, S.C. 29631. (803) 882-0268.

Texas

"Tut" Bartzen Tennis Camp
Texas Christian University, Fort Worth. Coed (11–18). 22 courts. 4:1 ratio. June 1–June 28. $235/6 days. Write: "Tut" Bartzen, Camp Director, 6008 Wallen Ave., Fort Worth, Tex. 76133. (817) 921-7960, 292-0242.

Vermont

All American Sports
Topnotch-at-Stowe, Stowe. Adults. 15 courts (4 indoor). 4:1 ratio. 3-, 4-, 5-, 7-day sessions. All year. From $195. Write: All American Sports, 366 Madison Ave., New York, N.Y. 10017. (212) 697-9220.

West Virginia

Fritz Schunck Tennis Camp

Bethany College, Bethany. Coed (9–17). 15 courts (3 indoor). 4:1 ratio. June 8–August 2. $285/week, $550/2 weeks. Write: Fritz Schunck, Camp Director, Washington Plaza, 1420 Centre Ave., Pittsburgh, Pa. 15219.

Wisconsin

Nick Bollettieri Tennis Camp

Wayland Academy, Beaver Dam. 15 courts (4 indoor). Coed (8–18). 3-week sessions. June 22–August 16. $290/week. Family weeks. July 27–August 16. Write: Gordon Kotinek, Camp Director, 1024 Lawndale Drive, Beaver Dam, Wis. 53916.

The Stap National Tennis Camp, Inc.

Carthage College, Kenosha, Wis. Coed (9–17). 24 courts (4 indoor). 5:1 ratio. 3-week sessions. June 15–July 25. Write: The Stap National Tennis Camp, Inc., 1328 Woodland Dr., Deerfield, Ill. 60015. (312) 945-4755.

France

Ramey Tennis Schools

Albi Tennis Club, Albi. Coed (12–18). 4 courts (1 indoor). 4:1 ratio. July 29–August 18. $725/3weeks. Write: Ramey Tennis Schools, Rte. #6, Owensboro, Ky. 42301. (502) 771-4723/5590.

The Nick Bollettieri Tennis Academy

Located in Sarasota, Florida, Nick's academy is a unique facility because it is a combination of academic institution and tennis camp. It offers nine months' education at a private school ($160 per month), a concentrated tennis program ($500 per month), and room and board ($350 per month) for a total approximate cost of $1,010 per month. The academy takes its pupils to tournaments; picks them up from individual residences and drives them to school, to the Colony Beach and Tennis Resort for practice on hard courts, and to the Bollettieri-DePalmer Club in Bradenton for prac-

tice on clay; takes them to dinner; tutors them; and chaper-
ones them at all times. Obviously, the academy is for the
serious player who wants to be totally immersed in tennis.
One measure of success for the program is that seventy-nine
of its students are already nationally ranked.

The Affluent Parent

One might say that Kathy May Teacher had a privileged
childhood. Daughter of David May, a May Company Department Store executive, Kathy grew up in Beverly Hills with
a tennis court and swimming pool in her backyard. Her
tennis career, started when she was three, has been an extremely successful one, including hundreds of junior titles
and numerous women's titles. Today, at twenty-three, she is
ranked seventeenth in the world. She was taught by such
renowned coaches as Pancho Segura, Tony Trabert, and
Robert Lansdorp, and even had a number of lesser pros as
practice partners. Kathy lacked for nothing. While this
might lead parents to conjure up an image of a spoiled, pampered brat, it isn't so. Kathy is and always has been an extremely polite, soft-spoken young lady, well-liked by her
peers. Although a fierce competitor, her court manners are
impeccable and her honesty and integrity beyond reproach.
How was it possible that Kathy escaped becoming a prima
donna?

According to David May, any parent, wealthy or poor, can
hurt his child. It's the parent's attitude that's important, not
his bank account. First of all, Mr. May never made it man-
datory that Kathy play tennis; that was always her choice.
What he did require of her, and all his children, was "that
they try and do *something* to the best of their ability so they
could feel proud of themselves. I told them they just couldn't
lie back in life. I want them to see how far they can go. But I
always made it very clear that it was just as important to be
a nice person as it was to win."

Mr. May's attitude is strikingly contrasted with the attitude of the wealthy father of one of Kathy's fellow competi-

tors. This domineering father emphasized a win-at-all-costs approach and proudly stated, "I don't want my child to win any sportsmanship award." Well, his wish came true. Not only did his daughter (who was an extremely promising, high-ranked junior player) not win any sportsmanship awards, but she was widely known as a cheater and temperamental person and was disliked by many of her peers. The girl can't be blamed, because she was responding to enormous parental pressures. In her young life it was much easier to cheat to win, rather than lose and face the wrath of her father. It was not an uncommon sight to see this girl after a loss publicly humiliated and slapped by her father. Obviously, tennis for this girl, despite her talents and many successes, was an extremely painful experience. As soon as she was free of her father's domination, she quit tournament tennis entirely.

This girl and Kathy May had very similar environments and backgrounds, but they developed totally different tennis attitudes and personalities, because of the different attitudes of their parents. In Mr. May's words, "I think kids need a lot of encouragement. People don't go very far without encouragement." He always stressed to his children that certain "ideas and standards of morals had to be upheld, and how you treat other people was important, not just winning." In fact, today, after all the accolades Kathy has won for her tennis abilities, what Mr. May seems most proud of is a sentence in a recent article on Kathy that states, "She has nice manners and looks good." Thus, Mr. May's foremost concern was to raise a happy, moral, decent person—an endeavor in which he has definitely succeeded.

"Advantages" of the Affluent Parent

Being able to afford expert coaching and a good deal of court time are the main advantages of the affluent parent. When money isn't a factor, a parent can hire the best coach available and buy as much court time as the child can use, or even build a court at home. Ten or fifteen years ago these were definite advantages, but they have become less so since the game has emerged from the exclusivity of clubs. Today, as discussed, there are a number of alternative facilities to clubs that are either free or inexpensive. Even in some clubs, junior programs include some children whose parents are unable to pay the full amount on scholarships or at minimal fees. Thus, kids of all socioeconomic strata are able to play as much as they want to.

It is still true that coaching can be costly, with some of the better-known coaches charging about $100 per hour, and they're probably worth it. However, these coaches aren't bloodless mercenaries; they are just responding to the law of supply and demand. They have only so many hours they can supply to students, and because there are many more students than hours, the price goes up. There are few coaches who would hesitate to teach a child for free, if that child was highly motivated and showed some promise. There is nothing more exciting for a coach than to see an eager child blossom under his guidance. This is gratification money can't buy. Besides, what coach doesn't dream of developing a Tracy Austin or Bjorn Borg whose court successes will focus the limelight on them?

Thus, the advantages of money that might have existed fifteen years ago are no longer as effective today. Fortunately, the game has widened its vistas and made it possible for anyone to play, regardless of his financial background.

The Pitfalls of the Affluent Parent

While there are no overwhelming advantages of wealth in the development of a child's tennis career, there are a number of pitfalls. A potentially disastrous one for parents is confusing money with love. Giving a child more material things does not replace true companionship, warmth, and affection, nor will it buy love from a child. How often have you heard a parent complain, "Why is my daughter always in trouble? I've given her everything she wanted." Everything, perhaps, but time and affection. Dressing a child in the latest, most expensive tennis clothes can't replace a half hour of parental time watching a son or daughter play and praising his or her efforts. Parents must be honest with themselves about why they are giving material things: to make a child love him more? to get rid of the child for a while? to assuage guilt feelings? to turn the child into a Martina Navratilova? or to make the child happy by helping him or her along a path the child has chosen?

Another pitfall of giving material things is that the more parents give, the more they may expect from the child. If parents give a child the best in lessons and equipment, then they may subconsciously expect the best tennis out of the child, even when he's not capable of it. Money can't buy talent or desire. Again, parents must examine their own motives. Do they want to have a little tennis star to fortify their own drooping self-esteem? Are they forcing things on their child "because they never had them as children?" Whatever their motives, they are inadvertently putting a great deal of pressure on their children. A child can be only what he is and can sense when parental expectations exceed what he can give, leading to a feeling of failure and alienation. Parents should give, but be sure it's without unreasonable expectations.

Two other minor pitfalls are that a plenitude of everything can take incentive and a sense of appreciation away from a child. In contrast to Mr. May, Kathy felt there were certain drawbacks to her financial status in life. "Everything was too easy and available. There was nothing to work for, so I never worked as hard as I could. I only realized this about four years ago. I'm much more appreciative now and realize how lucky I was and am."

Financial Help

If your child shows desire and promise in being a tournament player, and you are not financially capable of supporting his career, there are many sources of financial help through clubs, associations, and individual sponsors. Many

99

of the world's best players needed and were able to get financial help outside their family—Pancho Gonzales, Billie Jean King, and Rosie Casals, to name just three.

My parents were certainly not poor, but they had to adhere to a very tight budget and had no money for extravagant luxuries. They could afford only the minimum in tennis expenses for me and my brother. For a while we had lessons, but times got a little hard and they had to stop. By that time (a year or two after we started), we had shown enough interest and ability that our teacher (tennis great May Sutton Bundy) gave us free lessons, and my parents would pay when they could. This type of generosity is often found in the tennis world. A few years later, Constantin Tanasescu, a Rumanian Davis Cup player, also gave me free lessons. He would teach paying pupils at a public park from 7:00 A.M. to 7:00 P.M., then take me to a private tennis court with lights and give me an hour's free lesson at least once a week.

When I was ten years old, the Santa Monica Tennis Patrons started giving me $25 every summer to help pay for tournament entry fees. Then when I was sixteen and highly ranked in southern California, the Southern California Tennis Association gave me a few hundred dollars to help pay my way back east to play national tournaments. Even the Riviera Tennis Club, where I occasionally practiced but wasn't a member, raised money to help defray my expenses.

Mine is not an unusual story; in fact, it's quite the opposite. Many players have been helped in this way. A few have even had individual sponsors who would not only pay for all the usual expenses but send their player to exotic places like Australia for special training or practice. Therefore, if a child needs some financial help, contact the local tennis patrons group and regional tennis association and explain the situation. They have dealt with these problems many times before and will be able either to help directly or offer good suggestions.

What It All Costs

The following is a rough estimate we have worked out of the expenses for a serious tennis player over an eight-year period. We are focusing on the serious player because this would be the only case where expenses could become substantial. For the recreational player, expenses are much less. What follows is an itemized list of expenses for a young player starting at age ten, who is enthusiastic and has the ability to play tournaments. This hypothetical player is learning on public courts without court fees. (We hope that runaway inflation won't make the prices obsolete before this book goes into print!)

Expenses from Ages 10 to 18

First Year

The child is a beginner and the parents would like to give him a thorough introduction to the game.

Equipment

Racket with nylon string		$ 45
Shoes (2 pairs)		40
Shirts (2)		20
Shorts (2)		24
Balls, used (½ gross)		20
Restringing		15
	Equipment subtotal	$164

Lessons

Private ½ hour @ $12 (40)		$480
Clinics @ $6 (25)		150
	Lessons subtotal	$630
	First-year total	$794

Second Year

The student has increased his interest and is starting to play in some local and state tournaments.

Equipment

Rackets (2)	$ 90
Restringing	15
Shoes (3 pairs)	60

Balls, used (½ gross)		20
Clothes, including warm-up suit		200
	Equipment subtotal	$385
Lessons		
Private ½ hour @ $12 (52)		$ 624
Clinics @ $6 (104, 2/week)		624
	Lessons subtotal	$1,248
Tournaments		
Local, entry fees (3)		$ 18
State, entry, transportation, 2 days		
room and board (1)		120
U.S.T.A. card		10
	Tournament subtotal	$ 148
	Second-year total	$1,781

Third Year

The student is now reaching a B+ level of play and shows good promise in local tournaments.

Equipment		
Rackets with gut string (2)		$150
Restringing (2)		60
Clothes		200
Shoes (3 pairs)		60
Balls, new (½ gross)		80
	Equipment subtotal	$550
Lessons		
Same as second-year program		$1,248
Tournaments		
Local and state (4)		$ 300
U.S.T.A. card		10
	Tournament subtotal	$ 310
	Third-year total	$2,108

Fourth Year

Student receives a state ranking of 8 in the 14-and-under division. Parents, coach, and student are prepared to increase number of tournaments.

Equipment	
Same as third year	$ 550
Lessons	
Same as third year	$1,248

(continued)

(Expenses, continued)

Tournaments

Local, state, and national		$ 600
U.S.T.A. card		10
	Tournament subtotal	$ 610
	Fourth-year total	$2,408

Fifth Year

Student receives an excellent state ranking and his first national ranking. Because of these rankings, shoe and racket companies put student on a VIP list and supply him with free rackets. Pro sees excellent potential and does not charge for lessons.

Equipment

Gut (6 sets)		$ 190
Clothes		350
Balls, new (½ gross)		80
	Equipment subtotal	$ 620
Tournaments (travel, fees, U.S.T.A. card)		$1,200
	Fifth-year total	$1,820

Sixth Year

Same as fifth year	$1,820

Seventh Year

Student becomes an outstanding player. Student, parents, and coach decide to really go for the big tournaments. The main cost now is transportation. Room and board received free at many tournaments.

Travel, room, board, and entries	$3,000

Eighth Year

Student is ranked in the top four in the country. Number of tournaments again increased.

Travel, room, board, and entries	$5,000
Grand total for eight years	$18,731

One additional note. The student is now approached by twenty colleges and offered full scholarships. He or she either accepts a four-year full scholarship worth about $25,000 to $32,000 or goes on to play professional tennis, worth who knows what?

103

The Fifty Best Municipal Tennis Courts*

Club	Location	Courts	Other Data
Ala Moana Tennis Center	Honolulu, Hawaii	10 hard outdoor	Beautiful ocean view. Site of many state and sectional tournaments.
Albuquerque Tennis Complex	Albuquerque, N.M.	16 hard outdoor	$1 an hour for a reserved court keeps it filled morning, noon, and night.
Awbury Tennis & Recreation Center	Philadelphia, Pa.	12 hard outdoor	$2 a year gives unlimited play; special programs for inner-city youth.
Bridges Tennis Center	Jackson, Miss.	15 hard outdoor	A full-service tennis center in a country-club setting. Great pro shop.
H. E. Butt Municipal Tennis Center	Corpus Christi, Tex.	16 hard outdoor	Highly competitive junior program; twice host to NCAA championships.
Central Park Tennis Courts	New York, N.Y.	30 outdoor (26 clay, 4 hard)	A super tennis layout in a sylvan setting in the heart of Manhattan.
Cheviot Hills Tennis Complex	Los Angeles, Calif.	14 hard outdoor	In plush suburbia, a hotbed of high-class California-style tennis.

*©1979, *Tennis* Magazine, a New York Times Company. Reprinted with permission.

104

Club	Location	Courts	Other Data
Harold T. Clark Tennis Center	Cleveland, Ohio	9 hard outdoor	New 5,000-seat stadium expected to host Davis Cup, major pro tourney.
Dwight F. Davis Memorial Tennis Center	St. Louis, Mo.	19 hard outdoor	Named after the donor of the original Davis Cup; best in the area.
Deering Oaks Park	Portland, Me.	12 outdoor (8 clay, 4 hard)	First come, first served—and no charge—in picturesque New England.
Exeter Recreation Park	Exeter, N.H.	10 hard outdoor	Babysitting is no problem; there's a "tot lot" next to the court area.
Flamingo Park Tennis Courts	Miami Beach, Fla.	17 outdoor (13 clay, 4 hard)	Site of the prestigious Orange Bowl and Sunshine Cup junior tournaments.
Folsom Tennis Center	San Diego, Calif.	25 hard outdoor	Some say it's the best in the west; host to 13 big tournaments.
Gates Tennis Center	Denver, Colo.	20 hard outdoor	Everything you need for great tennis; modern clubhouse with all the niceties.

(continued)

The Fifty Best Municipal Tennis Courts (*continued*)

Club	Location	Courts	Other Data
Golden Gate Park Tennis Courts	San Francisco, Calif.	21 clay outdoor	A hacker's delight, but also famous for turning out top stars.
Bitsy Grant Tennis Center	Atlanta, Ga.	23 outdoor (13 clay, 10 hard)	3 stadium courts; host to 6 big tournaments. Old-time elegance.
Griffith Park–Vermont Canyon	Los Angeles, Calif.	12 hard outdoor	Bright and airy the year round; tennis program directed by Darlene Hard.
Holiday Park Tennis Center	Ft. Lauderdale, Fla.	20 outdoor (17 clay, 3 hard)	Where pro Jimmy Evert taught his daughter, Chris, everything she knows.
Indianapolis Sports Center	Indianapolis, Ind.	24 outdoor (18 clay, 6 hard)	Patterned after New York's National Tennis Center.
Ken Lake Tennis Center	Hardin, Ky.	5 hard outdoor, 4 hard indoor	Brand-new and bubbling over with activity; beautiful lakefront setting.
La Fortune Park Tennis Center	Tulsa, Okla.	12 hard outdoor	Part of a complete recreational complex; has hosted 3 big tournaments.

Club	Location	Courts	Other Data
Liberty Park Tennis Complex	Salt Lake City, Utah	16 hard outdoor	Big on junior instruction, junior leagues; courts free; complete rec center.
Longshore Tennis Courts	Westport, Conn.	9 clay outdoor	Part of fine sports complex overlooking Long Island Sound.
Louisville Tennis Center	Louisville, Ky.	9 clay outdoor	8,000-seat stadium; site of the Grand Prix Louisville Classic.
J. Spencer Love Tennis Center	Greensboro, N.C.	13 clay outdoor	Employs 30 full- and part-time pros in massive teaching program.
McFarlin Tennis Center	San Antonio, Tex.	22 hard outdoor	Park setting; 3 stadium courts; all amenities, including top pro shop.
Memorial Field Athletic Complex	Concord, N.H.	10 outdoor (5 hard, 5 clay)	Centerpiece of a complete rec complex; courts free, except at night.
Mobile Tennis Center	Mobile, Ala.	34 hard outdoor	A premier facility; well-kept and well-regulated; 4 stadium courts.
Joseph Moran Tennis Courts	Holland, Mich.	10 hard outdoor	Heavy on junior development, inter-clay rivalry. No charge for courts.

(continued)

The Fifty Best Municipal Tennis Courts (*continued*)

Club	Location	Courts	Other Data
Nicollet Tennis Center	Minneapolis, Minn.	11 hard outdoor	Active, year-round teaching program; 6 "bubble-tops" for winter play.
A. C. Nielsen Tennis Center	Winnetka, Ill.	12 hard outdoor, 8 indoor	Huge junior development program; teachers include all-time great George Lott.
North Central Community Tennis Center	Indianapolis, Ind.	21 hard outdoor, 6 hard indoor	2,000 youngsters in junior development program headed by top coach Bill Price.
North Fulton Tennis Center	Atlanta, Ga.	24 outdoor (14 hard, 10 clay)	Brand-new, full-service tennis center; big on junior development and league play.
Oklahoma City Tennis Center	Oklahoma City, Okla.	24 hard outdoor	Host to 4 big tournaments; with sunken courts for protection from wind.
Owl Creek Municipal Tennis Center	Virginia Beach, Va.	14 hard outdoor	Oceanfront setting; year-round junior program; 2 play areas for tots.
Phoenix Tennis Center	Phoenix, Ariz.	22 hard outdoor	Active junior program; has hosted U.S.T.A. district, sectional tourneys.

Club	Location	Courts	Other Data
Portland Tennis Center	Portland, Ore.	8 hard outdoor, 4 hard indoor	First municipal courts in Northwest; outstanding junior program.
Querbes Tennis Center	Shreveport, La.	10 outdoor (6 clay, 4 hard)	Louisiana's finest; pro shop with balcony over-looking all courts.
Randolph Tennis Center	Tucson, Ariz.	16 hard outdoor	Adding 8 new courts to accommodate booming instruction program.
Riverside Tennis Center	Wichita, Kans.	10 hard outdoor	Clubhouse, snack bar, lounge area and more—all in parklike setting.
Rock Creek Park	Washington, D.C.	22 outdoor (17 clay, 5 hard)	A top-notch facility; host to annual Washington Star tournament.
John Rogers Tennis Center	Memphis, Tenn.	25 hard outdoor	Already one of the largest in the U.S.; soon to add more courts.
Samuell Tennis Center	Dallas, Tex.	20 hard outdoor	One of the best junior programs in the nation; many players now ranked.
Seattle Tennis Center	Seattle, Wash.	2 hard outdoor, 10 hard indoor	Nice and new, with the first public indoor courts in the Seattle area.

(continued)

109

The Fifty Best Municipal Tennis Courts *(continued)*

Club	Location	Courts	Other Data
South Fulton Tennis Center	College Park, Ga.	24 outdoor (16 hard, 8 clay)	Big on instruction; only a year old and already host to 3 big tournaments.
Southwest Tennis Center	Houston, Tex.	26 hard outdoor	Full-service facility; heavy instruction; host to 2 big tourneys.
U.S.T.A. National Tennis Center	Flushing, N.Y.	25 hard outdoor, 9 hard indoor	New site of U.S. Open. A magnificent achievement by any standard.
Vancouver Indoor Tennis & Racquetball Center	Vancouver, Wash.	4 hard outdoor, 4 hard indoor	Financed entirely by municipal bonds to be repaid from court fees.
Joe White Tennis Center	Winston-Salem, N.C.	20 outdoor (14 clay, 6 hard)	Weekday rates—50 cents per person; big on ladders and league play.
Wilmette Park District— Centennial Park	Wilmette, Ill.	20 hard outdoor, 8 hard indoor	A pearl of a park on Chicago's North Shore; indoor time assigned by lottery.

The Fifty Best Indoor Clubs*

Club	Location	Courts	Other Data
Allaire Racquet Club	Wall, N.J.	6 cush. indoor, 4 hard outdoor	Extra-high ceilings, large pro shop, active social programs and a lot more.
Aspen Hill Racquet Club	Silver Spring, Md.	9 cush. indoor, 13 clay outdoor	Brand-new and beautiful; a country club for racquet sports.
Bellevue Athletic Club	Bellevue, Wash.	6 hard indoor, 5 hard outdoor	A total sports complex; in-house computer handles reservations.
Canyon Racquet Club	Salt Lake City, Utah	10 hard indoor, 13 hard outdoor	Programing for every member of the family; in the heart of the ski country.
Carmel Racquet Club	Carmel, Ind.	12 cush. indoor, 6 clay outdoor	Ladders, leagues, and tournaments among the many special dividends.
Cedardale Racquet Club	Haverhill, Mass.	12 cush. indoor, 25 outdoor	Innovative programs and a good blend of athletic and social activities.

(continued)

*© 1979, *Tennis* Magazine, a New York Times Company. Reprinted with permission.

The Fifty Best Indoor Clubs *(continued)*

Club	Location	Courts	Other Data
Columbus Indoor Tennis Club North	Columbus, Ohio	8 cush. indoor, 7 clay outdoor	One of the best junior programs around; low monthly dues and free court time.
The Courts	Oklahoma City, Okla.	7 cush. indoor, 4 hard outdoor	Host to several state tournaments; junior program includes summer camp.
East Hills Tennis Club	Grand Rapids, Mich.	14 cush. indoor, 4 hard outdoor	Castlelike exterior, friendly staff, year-round grand prix competition.
Evergreen Bath & Tennis Club	Evergreen Park, Ill.	11 cush. indoor	Big on instruction; huge center court has been the scene of several tourneys.
Four Seasons Tennis Club	Wilton, Conn.	10 clay indoor, 14 clay outdoor	Elegant club in lovely New England suburb; large junior program.
Franklin Racquet Club	Southfield, Mich.	20 hard indoor, 5 clay outdoor	One of the largest facilities around; includes all the niceties and then some.

Club	Location	Courts	Other Data
Hampshire Hills Health & Racquet Club	Milford, N.H.	6 cush. indoor, 6 clay outdoor	Complete health and racquet sports center; large, highly qualified staff.
Highpoint Racquet Club	Chalfont, Pa.	8 cush. indoor, 12 outdoor	Exquisite decor provides a contemporary setting; disco lounge, formal restaurant.
Holiday Tennis Club	Harvey, Ill.	8 cush. indoor, 7 cush. outdoor	Caters to more serious players; heavy tournament schedule, lots of league play.
Houston Indoor Tennis Club	Houston, Tex.	8 cush. indoor	First-rate club geared to adult players; full-time activities director.
Indian Creek Racquet Club	Overland Park, Kans.	9 cush. indoor, 9 clay outdoor	Handsomely decorated; skylights, racquetball, swimming are extra benefits.
Indianapolis Racquet Club	Indianapolis, Ind.	16 indoor (8 hard, 8 cush.), 8 clay outdoor	Granddaddy of the indoor game in the area; family oriented; inexpensive.

(continued)

The Fifty Best Indoor Clubs *(continued)*

Club	Location	Courts	Other Data
Lexington Tennis Club	Lexington, Ky.	10 cush. indoor, 10 hard outdoor	Fine management and pro staff; site of many sanctioned tournaments.
Louisville Tennis Club	Louisville, Ky.	12 cush. indoor, 14 hard outdoor	1,000-seat stadium court one of its many assets; an all-around facility.
Madison Racquet Club	Madison, Wis.	8 cush. indoor, 4 hard outdoor	Excellent playing conditions; top-flight management; minimal membership fee.
Meadow Creek Racquet Club	Lakewood, Colo.	7 cush. indoor, 3 hard outdoor	A premier club under the guidance of Cliff Buchholz; tastefully designed.
Mid-Town Tennis Club	Chicago, Ill.	18 cush. indoor	Considered by many to be the benchmark for indoor clubs.
Mid-Town Tennis Club	Rochester, N.Y.	16 cush. indoor	Offspring of Chicago's Mid-Town; center of organized tennis for the area.

Club	Location	Courts	Other Data
Mountain Park Racquet Club	Lake Oswego, Ore.	6 hard indoor, 6 hard outdoor	Tracy Austin won her first pro tourney here; one of the best pro shops.
Northwest Racquet & Swim Club	St. Louis Park, Minn.	14 cush. indoor	Membership fee entitles players to same privileges in 8 area clubs.
Overland Park Racquet Club	Overland Park, Kans.	14 cush. indoor, 8 hard outdoor	Award-winning architecture; a total facility with all the amenities.
Port Washington Tennis Academy	Port Washington, N.Y.	13 indoor (9 clay, 4 cush.), 3 hard outdoor	Primarily a tennis school for juniors; its graduates include Gerulaitis, McEnroe.
The Racquet Club	Natick, Mass.	11 cush. indoor	Wide range of programs for all ages and ability levels; ideal playing conditions.
The Racquet Club	Monroeville, Pa.	18 cush. indoor, 4 cush. outdoor	Huge center for racquet sports; sophisticated programs.

(continued)

The Fifty Best Indoor Clubs *(continued)*

Club	Location	Courts	Other Data
Racquet Club at Harper's Point	Cincinnati, Ohio	10 cush. indoor, 12 clay outdoor	A handsome facility with a nationally recognized teaching program.
Racquet Club at Ramblewood	Grandville, Mich.	8 cush. indoor, 4 clay outdoor	Competitive junior program; attracts both area families and local singles.
Radnor Racquet Club	Radnor, Pa.	6 cush. indoor	Wood interior, beamed ceilings, and excellent playing conditions.
Regency Racquet Club	McLean, Va.	6 cush. indoor, 13 cush. outdoor	Emphasis on instruction and league play. Many added attractions.
Rivercenter Tennis Club	New Orleans, La.	8 cush. indoor, 3 hard outdoor	Situated in the French Quarter; team tennis, leagues, and all that jazz.
San Francisco Tennis Club	San Francisco, Calif.	12 cush. indoor, 16 hard outdoor	Big and plush with outstanding playing conditions and lots of organized play.

Club	Location	Courts	Other Data
Saw Mill River Courts	Mt. Kisco, N.Y.	7 clay indoor, 10 clay outdoor	A cogeneration plant on premises to deal with energy crises.
Sioux Racquet Club	Sioux City, Iowa	8 cush. indoor, 4 clay outdoor	A broad-gauged facility with an enthusiastic staff; heavily into instruction.
Skyline Racquet & Health Club	Falls Church, Va.	7 cush. indoor	Hub of total fitness center; former British star Graham Stillwell is head pro.
Sound Shore Indoor Tennis	Port Chester, N.Y.	12 cush. indoor	A comfortable, walk-in facility that caters exclusively to the community.
Tennis World	Seattle, Wash.	23 hard indoor, 4 hard outdoor	Billed as the largest indoor club in the world; offers an array of programs.
Tennis World's Racquet World	Denver, Colo.	8 hard indoor, 9 hard outdoor	A complete athletic facility offering a full range of activities.

(continued)

The Fifty Best Indoor Clubs *(continued)*.

Club	Location	Courts	Other Data
Terminus Racquet Club	Atlanta, Ga.	7 cush. indoor, 16 outdoor	Frequently the site for conventions and large parties; animated atmosphere.
Town & Country Racquet Club	St. Louis, Mo.	11 cush. indoor, 12 hard outdoor	Country club ambience where tennis whites are in order; tri-level layout.
University Club	Houston, Tex.	10 cush. indoor	An exclusive, adult club situated above major shopping mall; business oriented.
Vantage Point Racquet Club	Allentown, Pa.	10 cush. indoor, 11 outdoor	Extremely attractive club; amenities include full-service restaurant.
West Hills Racquet Club	Portland, Ore.	6 hard indoor, 8 hard outdoor	Noteworthy junior development program; resort atmosphere with old-world charm.
Westroads Racquet Club	Omaha, Neb.	11 hard indoor, 4 hard outdoor	New, enthusiastic management promises to maintain the standard of excellence.

Club	Location	Courts	Other Data
Wimbleton Racquet Club	Memphis, Tenn.	15 hard indoor, 10 hard outdoor	Three full-time teaching pros, lots of league play.
Wood Lake Racquet Club	Sioux Falls, S.D.	6 cush. indoor, 4 cush. outdoors	A smaller facility, run with a big dose of enthusiasm; higher than usual ceilings.

The Fifty Best Outdoor Clubs*

Club	Location	Courts	Other Data
Agawam Hunt Club	E. Providence, R.I.	14 outdoor (12 grass, 2 clay)	Site of National Mother-Daughter Grass Court Championships.
Belle Mead Country Club	Nashville, Tenn.	12 outdoor (10 soft, 2 hard)	Site of Boy's 16 National Clay Court Championships.
Birchwood Club	Highland Park, Ill.	16 outdoor (12 soft, 4 hard)	So heavily used that there's a "starter" to direct court traffic.
Brookhaven Country Club	Dallas, Tex.	22 hard outdoor, 13 hard indoor	All courts lighted. Golf, swimming.
Brook Hollow Golf Club	Dallas, Tex.	12 hard outdoor	4 indoor courts under construction. Initiation: $12,000.
Camargo Club	Indian Hill, Ohio	9 outdoor (7 soft, 2 hard)	Badminton, golf, ice skating, trap shooting, fox hunting.
Chancellors Racquet Club	Houston, Tex.	10 hard outdoor, 10 hard indoor	Indoor courts are two-tone brown; 12 courts being added.

*©1979, *Tennis* Magazine, a New York Times Company. Reprinted with permission.

120

Club	Location	Courts	Other Data
Charlotte Country Club	Charlotte, N.C.	12 soft outdoor	Plantation-style club-house. Squash, golf, 5 swimming pools.
Chevy Chase Club	Chevy Chase, Md.	19 outdoor (15 soft, 4 hard)	Platform tennis, bowling, ice skating, golf.
Cleveland Racquet Club	Cleveland, Ohio	12 soft outdoor, 10 comp. indoor	Squash, platform tennis, indoor pool.
Cleveland Skating Club	Cleveland, Ohio	11 comp. outdoor, 4 comp. indoor	Ice skating, curling, plat-form tennis. Initiation: $3,750.
Country Club of Detroit	Detroit, Mich.	10 soft outdoor	Platform tennis, swim-ming, and one of nation's top 100 golf courses.
Country Club of Virginia	Richmond, Va.	20 outdoor (11 soft, 9 hard)	Golf (45 holes), platform tennis, swimming.
Creve Coeur Racquet Club	St. Louis, Mo.	15 outdoor (9 hard, 6 soft)	Built by a restauranteur and especially noted for dining facilities.
Dallas Country Club	Dallas, Tex.	14 outdoor (8 soft, 6 hard)	Golf, swimming, bridge, aerobic dancing, exercise classes.

(continued)

The Fifty Best Outdoor Clubs *(continued)*

Club	*Location*	*Courts*	*Other Data*
Germantown Cricket Club	Philadelphia, Pa.	45 outdoor (27 grass, 18 soft)	Bill Tilden's home club. Site of Men's Senior Championships.
Houston Racquet Club	Houston, Tex.	41 outdoor (21 hard, 20 soft)	Site of Women's 35 Championships. Initiation: $5,000.
Longwood Cricket Club	Chestnut Hill, Mass.	41 outdoor (25 grass, 16 clay)	A Boston institution. Site of first Davis Cup match, in 1900.
Los Angeles Tennis Club	Los Angeles, Calif.	17 hard outdoor	All the greats have played here. Also, mecca of California junior tennis.
Los Caballeros Racquet Sports Club	Fountain Valley, Calif.	22 hard courts	20 racquetball courts, 18 more tennis courts planned.
Louisville Boat Club	Louisville, Ky.	18 outdoor (16 soft, 2 hard)	On Ohio River. Members frequently tie up in houseboats for days.
Meadow Club	Southampton, N.Y.	29 outdoor (25 grass, 4 hard)	Members include ex-Wimbledon champ Sidney B. Woods.

Club	Location	Courts	Other Data
Merion Cricket Club	Haverford, Pa.	40 outdoor (24 grass, 16 comp.)	Once a big stop on the summer circuit. Site of Men's 21-and-under.
Mission Hills Country Club	Palm Springs, Calif.	13 hard outdoor	Site of American Airlines Games and Colgate Series final.
New Haven Lawn Club	New Haven, Conn.	8 soft outdoor	Perhaps most elegant of all. A favorite of affluent Yalies.
New Orleans Country Club	New Orleans, La.	12 outdoor (9 soft, 3 hard)	Sugar Bowl host. Also, sponsors 60-player traveling junior squad.
Newport Beach Tennis Club	Newport Beach, Calif.	19 hard outdoor	Styled after Forest Hills. Members include Roy Emerson.
Onwentsia Club	Lake Forest, Ill.	10 soft outdoor, 2 comp. indoor	Indoor building won American Institute of Architects award.
Orange Lawn Tennis Club	South Orange, N.J.	20 outdoor (12 grass, 8 soft)	Old, elegant, exclusive. Site of former warm-up for U.S. Open.

(continued)

The Fifty Best Outdoor Clubs *(continued)*

Club	Location	Courts	Other Data
Paradise Valley Country Club	Paradise Valley, Ariz.	10 hard outdoor	Touring umpire Mike Blanchard was tennis pro here 1960–1972.
Philadelphia Country Club	Gladwyn, Pa.	8 soft outdoor	Trap, skeet, squash, platform tennis, golf, swimming.
Philadelphia Cricket Club	Philadelphia, Pa.	47 outdoor, 3 comp. indoor	35 grass courts are most in U.S. Site of Girls' 18 Nationals.
Piedmont Driving Club	Atlanta, Ga.	8 outdoor (7 soft, 1 hard)	"Old South" in style, taste and atmosphere. Initiation: $4,500.
Piping Rock	Locust Valley, N.Y.	16 outdoor (12 soft, 4 hard)	Ultra-exclusive. Amid towering pines and rolling horse country.
Ponte Vedra Club	Ponte Vedra, Fla.	15 soft outdoor	Site of USPTA Clay Court Championships.
Racquet Club of Memphis	Memphis, Tenn.	28 outdoor (16 soft, 12 hard)	Built on site of old Memphis Athletic Club. Site of U.S. Indoor.
Racquet Club of Palm Springs	Palm Springs, Calif.	12 hard outdoor	Where the stars play. Built by actors Charlie Farrell, Ralph Bellamy.

Club	Location	Courts	Other Data
Regency Racquet Club	McLean, Va.	13 comp. outdoor, 6 comp. indoor	Racquetball, squash, platform tennis, swimming.
River Hills Country Club	Jackson, Miss.	26 outdoor (20 soft, 6 hard)	Site of Southern Senior Clay Court Championships.
River Oaks Country Club	Houston, Tex.	18 outdoor (10 soft, 8 hard)	Traditional tournament site; now hosts WCT event.
Riviera Country Club	Pacific Palisades, Calif.	19 hard outdoor	Super tennis layout plus one of nation's top twenty golf courses.
St. Louis Country Club	St. Louis, Mo.	8 outdoor (5 clay, 3 hard)	Platform tennis, ice skating, horseback riding, golf, swimming.
Seattle Tennis Club	Seattle, Wash.	13 hard outdoor, 6 hard indoor	Oldest, finest in Northwest, with dock space for members' yachts.
T Bar M	Dallas, Tex.	20 hard outdoor, 8 indoor	Founded by, named for, Jack Turpin, Tut Bartzen, C. Mabry.
Town Club	Fox Point, Wis.	18 outdoor (15 soft, 3 hard)	Former site National Clay Court Championships, Westerns.

(continued)

The Fifty Best Outdoor Clubs *(continued)*

Club	*Location*	*Courts*	*Other Data*
University Club	Memphis, Tenn.	14 outdoor (8 soft, 4 hard, 2 comp.)	Second oldest club in Memphis. Adding 8 courts.
WCT Peachtree World of Tennis	Norcross, Ga.	18 outdoor (16 hard, 2 soft)	A Lamar Hunt facility. Calls itself "finest private tennis club in U.S."
Westchester Country Club	Rye, N.Y.	24 outdoor (18 soft, 6 grass)	Enormous facility with massive Tudor clubhouse.
West Side Tennis Club	Forest Hills, N.Y.	48 outdoor	Former site of U.S Open, was symbol of U.S. tennis the world over.
Woodstock Club	Indianapolis, Ind.	9 soft outdoor	Former site, National Clay Court Championships.

TENNIS CAN be played at a variety of places for a variety of costs. Where a family lives and how serious a player a child is will be strong influences on how costly tennis will be. If some time is spent researching possible facilities and possible sources of financial help, tennis need not be a financial burden to parents.

7.

Coaching

What Is a Coach?

A coach or tennis teacher is much more than just a teacher of tennis. In Nick's words, "Being a mother, father, friend, foe, guide, leader, and psychologist are just some of the roles I have to play as a coach. I have to prove to each student that I really care and feel every win and loss with them, but I have to be more detached than a parent, especially in the face of a loss. When a student loses, it's very important to maintain or even increase his or her motivation, which I can do by pointing out specific things the student did well." Fundamentally, then, a coach is a surrogate parent with more objectivity than a real parent, and an expert in the area of tennis.

Why Have a Coach?

One important function of a coach is to teach children the proper fundamentals of tennis. Tennis is a game of complex motor skills requiring coordination, timing, and strength. Bad technique can be very damaging in that it can severely limit the amount of progress a player can make. Many youngsters have a natural feel for the game and can actually play, but this does not guarantee good technique. Learning to stroke the ball properly may take extra time and effort at first, but it pays great dividends in the long run. Thus, a coach can make sure a child starts out on the right foot.

Qualities of a Good Coach

The qualities to look for in a good coach are in two general areas: his or her personal characteristics, and his or her expertise in tennis. In the area of personal qualities, ideally a good coach should be understanding, dedicated, compassionate, patient, and caring. By having these overlapping qualities, the coach then gains the emotional trust of the student, and a very special relationship is established. In discussing the understanding a coach should have, Nick says:

A coach has to learn the idiosyncrasies of his or her students—know when to be positive and when to be negative. There are certain students who have to be hit over the head with a hammer. There are students you can take aside and talk to in a calm voice. Then there are students on a tennis court who have to really be pushed verbally and almost embarrassed in order to bring out their qualities. Sometimes viewers from the sidelines say, "How in the world can a coach push a young boy or girl like that?" Perhaps the viewer doesn't understand that this coach has been with the student a long time and has come to know the student on a very personal basis, and because of that, he knows how to bring out the best in the student.

The dedication that most good coaches have is obvious in Nick. He knows all his students very well and knows what they're like as people off and on the court. Nick travels with the students who play tournaments to give them extra support and to see how they play under match conditions. He teaches from 7:00 A.M. to 7:00 P.M., almost nonstop, and loves it. Off the court his mind is still on the game and his pupils, not out of duty but because he truly loves what he is doing. This type of devotion to tennis and teaching gives each student a feeling of uniqueness and self-worth, which leads to a special rapport between student and coach. When this kind of relationship is established, the student will push far beyond his normal level of proficiency by fighting and concentrating more and giving 110 percent. This is the student's way of showing Nick that he appreciates what Nick is doing for him.

The other general area of qualities one looks for in a coach is his expertise in tennis. Teaching tennis has changed a great deal, because the game itself has changed. No longer is a basic knowledge of the fundamental strokes sufficient; thorough teaching knowledge of all the varieties of spins, strategies, and specialty shots is also needed. Along with being able to use the latest techniques in teaching stroke production and court strategy, a coach must be well versed in teaching physical fitness and health maintenance. Whether a child is going to be a serious player or not, a good coach can help a child learn good lifelong health and fitness habits. Because of the variety of rackets, strings, balls, and shoes available, a coach can help select the equipment that is best suited to a child's game and abilities. Thus, a coach must be up to date with the latest in tennis goods, both soft (clothes) and hard (racket). Another requirement of a good coach is that he be familiar with the current junior competitions, locally and nationally. If a child has any tournament aspirations, the coach should be able to inform a child what he is up against, and then help him train accordingly.

When all these qualities come together in a coach, and this coach has a pupil who can profit by, use, and appreciate these qualities to the optimum, then a relationship similar to Nick's and Brian Gottfried's is formed. Today, Brian at age thirty is ranked number 16 in the world (although he has been ranked as high as number 3), has played in Davis Cup competition for the United States, and has had an outstanding tennis record in both singles and doubles. Although he has been helped and coached by several people (like Dennis Ralston and Tony Trabert on the Davis Cup Team), Brian has said, "I owe the foundation of my game to Nick Bollettieri." When Brian was ten he essentially became part of Nick's family, living with him on and off for the next eight years. The relationship between Nick and Brian was more like father and son than coach and pupil. Nick and Brian would get up and be on the court working out by 7:00 A.M., both equally eager and enthusiastic, in strictly a labor of love. Brian went everywhere with Nick, caught minutes on the court with him here and there, and, in Nick's words, repaid him by "working hard, always being humble and polite, and never saying a mean word." Obviously, this arrangement worked to the benefit of both men. Brian was given a solid foundation in tennis, and Nick was given the immeasurable satisfaction of helping Brian become the great player he is.

The Relationship between Coach and Pupil

Because of the close relationship that's usually established between pupil and coach, parents shouldn't expect their child always to come home happy from a lesson. I can't tell you how often as a child I was reduced to tears on the court by Mrs. Bundy (who I loved like a grandmother and in fact called Granny). Jeanne Austin can recall many times when Tracy and Robert Lansdorp, Tracy's coach, had battles during lessons, leaving her in tears. The reason for this is that children don't know how much they can give of themselves physically or mentally until they are actually forced to do so, and the process of expanding can sometimes be downright painful. But it's part of the learning process, and the boost to a child's self-esteem when he ends up giving that extra 10 percent he thought was impossible will be well worth the pain.

On the whole, though, the relationship between pupil and coach should be fairly smooth, happy, and fun for the child. A child will grow to be very fond of his coach and quite trusting in all matters that concern tennis. A child will see his coach as the ultimate tennis authority, which can sometimes lead to problems between parents and the coach, especially if the parents have definite ideas about their child's tennis career.

The Relationship between Coach and Parent

Charlie Pasarell's parents are both excellent players with strong opinions concerning his tennis. Charlie remembers:

> My mother would fight with my coach, Welby van Horn, all the time over everything—whether she had the court reserved, whether I had enough time to play, or whether Welby was spending enough time with me. Yet they've always been very close, that's why they can fight. Once I said to my mother, "Well, mother, if you really think Welby was wrong, I won't take lessons from him anymore." She got really mad at me and said, "As far as tennis is concerned, you listen to Welby. Welby is the bible of tennis and anything he says, do. Don't listen to me." She was smart enough to realize that Welby was the real expert.

The relationship between coach and parent can be very emotional and complex.

In his many years of teaching children and dealing with parents, Nick has found certain methods especially helpful. He likes to have frequent chats with parents in order to hear what their goals and expectations are for their child, and to explain what he in turn thinks the child is capable of. Sometimes his views and those of the parents can be divergent, and he has to be brutally honest. In his own words,

> Parents often think their child can do a lot more, or are unwilling to admit that their child is limited in this particular sport. The parents just put blinders on their eyes—they will not accept this. So I think the relationship between coach and parent should be a very honest one. They should trust and be frank with each other. The relationship should not be one in which the coach is pacifying the parents by saying, "Oh, your daughter will be terrific," when the coach knows darn well the child won't be terrific. I think in most instances you gain more respect if you are honest and say, "I could be wrong, but I think your daughter has this ability. She will be able to play high

school tennis, and perhaps with a lot of work and dedication make a college team. But to attain a tennis scholarship, or become a touring professional, in my opinion, is very remote."

True, you may lose some parents who will take their students away, but in the long run I'm convinced that being extremely honest is the best way. Some parents feel I lack finesse, but I don't want to take any chances that they may not understand me, because the person getting hurt at the end is the child, not the parents.

Along with open and honest communications between coach and parents, parental noninterference is an important element in the relationship between coach and parent. Even if it's just one simple lesson a week, the parent, no matter what they know of the game, must try to understand that they are putting their child in the hands of a teaching professional they have selected. They have chosen this person and must give him a chance to show them that he can bring forth the hitting techniques, the running techniques, or whatever is necessary to make the student a player.

A top South African player and now teaching professional to many of the top juniors in the Philadelphia area describes how frustrating it is to have an interfering parent.

I have this young girl who's quite good, but not as good as her mother would like her to be. She works terribly hard, but I can't tell if it's because she likes the game or because her mother pushes her, because I've literally never had a chance to talk to her alone. Her mother is always there during lessons, during practice, during clinics, all the time. Once during a lesson the mother left the court to get something out of the car, and I quickly asked the child if she liked tennis. She said yes, but it's still hard for me to know for sure.

Anyway, I continued working with this girl, but from time to time her strokes would suddenly change. One week we were working on a topspin backhand, and the next week she came back with a slice! I found out that the mother had seen a sequence photo of Ken Rosewall's slice backhand and decided that's how her daughter was going to hit hers! Well, I made it very clear that I couldn't teach under those conditions and the mother should leave the child's strokes entirely alone. For the time being, things are okay, but I have my doubts. I'll probably have to stop teaching her.

Thus, the key elements in the relationship between coach and parents are open communications, clear understanding of goals and expectations, the parents' and the coach's, complete honesty, trust, and noninterference.

How to Choose a Coach

Besides the qualities discussed regarding a good coach (expertise, understanding, dedication, patience, and caring), there are also other criteria to help you choose a coach for your child. There are two organizations in the United States that test and certify tennis instructors, the U.S. Professional Tennis Association and the Professional Tennis Registry U.S.A. Although being certified by these organizations is no guarantee of excellence, it is a guideline to show that certain minimum teaching requirements have been met. Each organization tests applicants on and off the court on such matters as teaching theories, merchandising knowledge, and playing skills.

Whether or not a pro is certified, the best way of evaluating his abilities is by watching some lessons and by word of mouth. Here are some qualities to look for.

Does the pro have a nice "courtside manner"? Every beginner or new student is somewhat nervous when first going to a pro. The pro should be positive and be able to relax the student in order to create a good learning environment. Teaching should be done with a majority of positive comments, not negative ones.

Is the pro organized, both on and off the court? Does the lesson follow a logical progression? Is it obvious what the

134

pro is trying to convey to the pupil? Do lessons start and end pretty much on time, or are things a bit chaotic? Does the pro ask the student to do only those things that are within the student's capabilities?

Is the pro a competent player? The pro does not have to be a world-class player, by any means, but it is necessary that he be able to demonstrate the variety of strokes and spins that are being taught today.

Is the lesson fun for both pro and student? A good teacher loves teaching, has fun doing it, and conveys that feeling to the pupil. Some lessons are harder work than others, but learning a sport should be mostly fun, not work.

Is the pro active? Or does he just stand in one spot and drone on for a half hour? The concentration span of children is not great, so a pro must be an active participant in the lesson, changing drills and inventing games to keep the pupil's attention level high.

Has the pro developed competent players? Look at the caliber of student the pro attracts as well as the ones he develops. A pro doesn't have to be the coach of some hotshot student, but if the pro's students have smooth strokes and are capable of playing at a level that is fun for them, then the pro is doing an adequate job.

If parents are just beginning to learn about the game and aren't sure of their abilities to choose the right coach, they should seek advice and do the best they can. Mistakes aren't uncommon and certainly aren't irrevocable. If after about ten hours of lessons a child is not having fun or not showing some progress, a new coach might be in order. Parents should discuss their child with the pro, watch the pro teach again, and then reevaluate the situation.

How Much Coaching?

As Nick says,

No one can say how much coaching is required. There are students who just seem to pick up new additions to their game with very little difficulty. And, in turn, there are those who require hours and hours and hours of practice in order to develop the same technique that another student did in three or four minutes.

So the amount of coaching needed will often vary, and if one coach tells you that one lesson is enough, another says three, and another seven, they can all be right. But you can't come out and say, "This is it." So, on this particular point, I must say that the amount of coaching will vary according to the ability of the student and the heights the student will want to attain.

Keeping this information in mind, a minimum amount of coaching would be one half hour per week for the beginner. Students who may be more serious about the game might take two half-hour lessons per week and participate in one group clinic. Also, the number of lessons a child may want to take may vary with the seasons, with more lessons in the spring and summer than in the fall or winter. It should be kept flexible, but with any less than one lesson per week, a child can develop too many bad habits between lessons.

How long should a child take lessons? Again, the answer to this will vary a great deal from child to child. Basically, a child should take lessons as long as the interest and enjoyment are there and it is not a financial burden on the parents, because tennis is a game of never-ending learning. Touring pros are constantly checking in with their coaches to straighten out various problems or make certain improvements in their games. They even seek help from one another. In a recent tournament, Chris Evert spotted something wrong in Martina Navratilova's serve and helped her correct it. Martina went on to beat Chris in the finals with the help of her new, improved serve!

How Much It Costs

The cost of lessons will vary according to location and type of facility. A lesson in Terre Haute, Indiana, is probably not as expensive as one in La Costa, California. Also, lessons at resorts and clubs will be more expensive than those given at schools or in public parks. On the whole, though, a private half-hour lesson will cost about $12 to $15. Of course, the better-known teaching pros like Nick, Pancho Segura, Dennis Van Dermeer, and others will charge considerably more, around $35 a half hour.

Should Parents Teach Their Children?

Although there are many pros and cons regarding parents teaching their children, we feel that, for the most part, the disadvantages outweigh the advantages. Yes, it is true that there are some well-known "success" cases, like Jimmy Evert and Chris, Gloria Connors and Jimmy, Alex Mayer and Sandy and Gene, and Vitas Gerulaitis, Sr., and Vitas— but in each one of these cases, the parent is an extremely experienced teaching pro. Because the relationship between a coach and student is very complex and can be emotionally charged, it is important for the coach to remain somewhat detached and objective—a hard task for a parent, even if that parent has a great deal of tennis expertise. Billie Jean King, in her book with Greg Hoffman, *Tennis Love,* flatly states, "It's my firm belief that parents should refrain from teaching tennis to their children."

Teaching your child tennis is somewhat analogous to playing mixed doubles with a spouse. When it goes well, it can be a great deal of fun. But when it doesn't, it can lead to silly bickering, hurt feelings, and alienation. Nick discusses teaching his daughters:

> I enjoy working with my two daughters, but I can honestly say that, although I become very much a part of them when they play in a tournament, I have never, ever pushed, ridiculed, or embarrassed them. I just want them to play and have a good time. That may be hard for readers to believe, but I've seen too many parents alienate their children from them because of their overinvolve-

ment in the child's sport. There is no sport in the world worth risking hard feelings with my children or alienating them from me.

On the positive side of a parent's teaching a child are that it is a shared activity and thus can bring parent and child closer to each other, and it's cheaper. On the negative side, parent and child may get too emotional; conflicts on the court may be taken home, and vice-versa; the parent risks antagonizing and alienating the child. Overall, it just seems safer and simpler to entrust a good coach with teaching a child tennis. As Mrs. Austin says, "Tracy and Robert [her coach] really go at it, and sometimes Tracy yells and cries. I wouldn't want to get involved in that kind of relationship. I wouldn't take the risk of coaching—better to get a coach."

Although a parent's being a child's coach is not advised, a parent can still be a helper and practice partner. Tony Trabert recalls receiving help from his nontennis-playing father.

He would drive me ten miles out to the club to take lessons. He'd sit and watch and listen, and then later when I was practicing, he'd say, "Remember what Earl said about keeping your racket back," or whatever. He was learning by listening. He didn't say, "I told you to get your racket back." He'd say, "Remember what the coach said," so that it wasn't coming from him in my eyes, because I might have felt that he wasn't knowledgeable about the game.

On the other hand, Billie Jean King has a different point of view. In her book *Tennis Love,* she says,

I also feel that parents should not hang around to watch their children's lessons. Parents who take an active interest in their child's tennis development are to be applauded, but hovering around the court while a lesson is in progress may severely inhibit or distract a young player. The child will be less self-conscious if Mom or Dad disappear when the lesson begins, and the instructor will be more effective if he or she is dealing with a tennis student whose attention is not divided.

How your child reacts to a parent during a lesson or practice session is important. If the child is obviously nervous, distracted, and always sneaking glances at his parent, it probably would be better if the parent disappeared. On the other hand, if a child's composure and concentration seem unaltered by a parent's presence and if mother or father want to stay to listen and learn, then go ahead and try it. Parents may even be able to offer helpful reminders during one of the child's practices. However, if these remarks meet with any resistance, parents should just forget about them and let the coach do all the reminding and teaching.

HAVING A COACH is important physically and emotionally to a child. A coach can give a child a good start in the game so that there are no technical obstacles to his improvement. A coach, through understanding and positive reinforcement, can keep tennis fun for a child and help develop his self-esteem. In order to do the job right, the coach should have an open and honest relationship with the parents, so that they don't work at cross-purposes and all decisions are made for the ultimate benefit of the child. Since a coach can be a highly significant figure in a child's life, parents must take the time to learn how to choose a good one.

8.

Coaching Tips for Mind and Body

All the technical coaching in the world cannot turn a child into a good player or make tennis fun unless he has the right mental attitude. In this respect tennis can be an invaluable vehicle to teach a child how to develop a favorable mental outlook and demonstrate how this outlook can serve him in other endeavors. Only after a discussion of the mental aspects of learning will we discuss technical coaching tips, because only with a good mental attitude can technical advice be used to its fullest advantage.

Mental Attitude

The word *attitude* is bandied about quite frequently within sports circles, but what exactly does it mean? Is a "good" attitude always thinking "positive" thoughts? Is it an instinctual quality, or can one consciously change one's mental attitude?

Mental attitude is simply a person's reaction to life's events. Events in themselves are neither good nor bad, positive nor negative; it is our reactions to events that are positive or negative. A backhand volley comes over the net to Billie Jean King and she licks her chops and thinks, "Oh, boy! I got her now!" A backhand volley comes over the net to Clara Clumsy, who gasps, tenses up, and thinks, "Oh, no! She's got me now!" In these two instances the "event," a small sphere traveling over a net, was the same, only the two women's "reactions" to it were different. In the first case, Billie Jean was focused and alert, yet relaxed. Consequently, her eyesight was sharp and her reflexes and body primed for action, increasing her chances of making a good shot. In the second case, Clara's attitude will probably help fulfill her negative prophecy. Her reaction caused her body to become overly tense, which constricted her vision, slowed her reflexes, and lessened her chances of making a good shot. As the Greek Stoic philosopher Epictetus said, "Men are disturbed not by the things that happen, but by their opinion of the things that happen."

The key to a good attitude is not necessarily to see everything as positive, or through rose-colored glasses, but to see things as they really are, not as what you think they are. Ideally, a player will see a "neutral" ball coming over the net, neither a "good" nor a "bad" shot. The player can then make the necessary adjustments to prepare to hit the shot back. If the player sees an "Oh, boy!" shot coming over the net, he may get too excited, become overconfident, lose concentration, and make an error. On the other hand, if the player sees an "Oh, no!" shot coming, he may tense up and miss the shot. If the player can realize that the ball coming over the net is just a neutral event, then he is more capable of receiving and processing all the vital information gained from his senses, and of responding accordingly.

An example of a good mental attitude is the little girl who was asked if she could play the guitar. When she answered in the affirmative, her older brother said indignantly, "No, you can't! You've never played!" Whereupon she replied, "I know I haven't played, so how do I know I can't?" The little girl had no evidence that she could or couldn't play the guitar, so she just assumed she could. Many people when trying something for the first time, especially a sport, assume they can't do it. This assumption or mental attitude all but assures their failure. They have taken a neutral event, turned it into a negative one, and created a huge obstacle for themselves. As Nick says:

One of the most frustrating things for a coach to encounter is a child with a defeatist attitude. I hate to hear

141

comments from pupils like, "I can't do that," or "Gee, they're so good, I'll never be that good." I won't tolerate the words "I can't." I don't care if they can or can't, just as long as they try to the best of their ability. Forget the score—that's completely academic to the whole thing. All coaches and parents should require from students is that they *try*.

If mothers and fathers and coaches used this philosophy, I feel the results from the students would exceed expectations because the pressure is not on the students to always win. I can't stress enough that the worst loss can be a win if the student learns something and at the same time tries to the best of his ability and never gives up. That's what sports is all about.

Reprogramming

Fortunately, mental attitude is not an instinct but a learned behavior, and as such can be unlearned and relearned. In other words, our mental attitude can be reprogrammed. Our general mental outlook is the result of the information we select from the real world, just as a computer's output is the result of the specific data fed to it. If we choose to feed our computer (the brain) only half the information available from the real world, we can't expect to be able to act in a successful manner except by chance. For example, let's say you're driving your car on an extremely cold day. It starts to rain. If you just looked at your windshield and saw the rain bouncing off, you would drive your car in a way that was appropriate for wet roads. If you took in more information and looked beyond the windshield to the road, you might notice the rain freezing on the road, creating a dangerous driving situation. Your driving tactics would then be entirely different.

This example may seem simplistic and obvious, but in tennis, people often do not look beyond their windshields. A player sees a ball hit hard to his forehand side and thinks, "Oh my gosh, my forehand is weak and the ball was hit so hard!" In his fear or negative reaction, the player has just selected a portion of the available information (velocity and direction) to feed his computer—of course he's probably going to miss the shot. Another player may not have any emotional reaction to the same shot, and consequently notice not only the speed and direction of the ball but also the spin and wind velocity and direction, giving his "computer" more data to process and himself a much better chance of hitting the ball back.

Reprogramming Hints

There are several things a player can do on the court to reprogram himself so that he won't react negatively to neutral events. Here is some direct advice for a child that a parent can help convey to him or her.

1. *Stay in the "here-and-now."* You can do only one thing at a time and deal only with an event that is happening *now*. If you see a shot and think, "Oh no, a backhand. I can't hit it!" you're projecting yourself into the future and forecasting an outcome (which, through lack of useful data, you will proceed to fulfill). If you see a shot and think resignedly, "Oh no, another backhand," you are dwelling in the past and remembering your past backhand errors. On the other hand, if you focus on what is happening right now—the speed, spin, direction of the ball, the wind, the sun, your opponent's position on court, your position, and so on—and have total awareness of your surroundings, you won't have time to prejudge the event. That's why so much emphasis is put on watching the ball in tennis; it's a way of casting out all extraneous thoughts and reactions and staying concentrated on the here and now.
2. *Have an end result in mind.* The human body is an amazingly intricate and sophisticated piece of machinery. You walk into a room and want to turn the lights on. You look at the switch, raise your arm, and flip the

switch. You don't have to instruct yourself, "Okay, I'm two feet from the wall. Contract my deltoid muscle to raise my arm; now flex my forearm muscles; now contract my index finger to flip the switch." On the contrary, you just have to have an end result in mind, and your body will do the rest. The complexities are exponentially multiplied in tennis. A ball about two inches in diameter travels through the air at various speeds, spins, and directions, while you're moving at various speeds and directions, and you're able to hit this ball and place it pretty much where you want it to go with a racket that extends from your arm 27 inches and has about eighty-eight square inches of hitting surface! Amazing! If you had to direct your muscles consciously to carry out all the necessary movements, you would probably short circuit your brain! All you basically, consciously had to do was say, "I want to hit the ball back there," and the rest was taken care of by your body.

Your body is able to accomplish what your mind instructs it to do through the images your mind holds of the end result. You visualize turning the light switch on and you do it. In tennis you should always try to visualize where you want the ball to go. Luckily, because the court doesn't move, you can keep an image of the end result of a shot in your mind while still attending to the flight of the ball, in order to gather as much information as possible. In other words, if you want a shot to go crosscourt, you don't have to look there; the court is right where it was when you started. You might glance at the desired target area, then go back to paying full attention to the ball until you make contact. As an experiment, take a bath towel out to the court and place it in the service court of your opponent's side. From your serving position, look at the towel, knowing you want to hit it. Now toss the ball and serve it, without taking your eye off the ball until your racket has struck it. You will be surprised how often you hit the towel—and it will seem relatively effortless. What you have done in this exercise is to establish a specific end result, staying in the here and now by doing one thing at a time, which was simply focusing on the ball, and the ball only, throughout the serve.

Often in a game situation a difficult shot will come over the net, the player will panic, and the thought and image of missing the ball will flash through his mind. It's no surprise, then, that the body simply follows its orders and misses the ball. Remember to program your computer with the data you want it to follow, not with the data you don't want. Thus, it's helpful always to instruct yourself in the positive, not the negative. For example, how often in a tense situation have you stood up to the line and adamantly ordered yourself not to double fault, and bingo, you double faulted? Your body, like a good soldier, just followed the orders given by you inadvertently through the image of a double fault. Instead, in a similar situation, think of where specifically you want the ball to go, then let your body follow those positive orders.

3. *Do not be afraid of making mistakes.* One of the main learning methods is trial and error. By going ahead and trying to do something, making mistakes, and then making corrections, people learn a desired behavior. To use this method effectively, you must use all possible feedback, both positive and negative. In this way a negative can be turned into a positive, because you can use that negative "error" information to make corrections.

If you hit a forehand outside the court knowing exactly where it did land will help you make adjustments for future forehands. Often a player will miss a shot, groan, "Oh, no!," squeeze his eyes shut, and turn away. By not looking at his errors, this player is eliminating half the valuable information available to fine tune his game. Mistakes are a necessary part of tennis, learning, and life; use them properly for your benefit. The great

145

Babe Ruth at one time held the all-time record for the most home runs—but also the all-time record for the most strikeouts.

4. *Admit your mistakes.* You are only human. Accept the fact that you're going to make mistakes, that everything isn't going to be positive, that you will have bad feelings, but that you can learn from these "negatives." Remember, you can use this negative feedback to produce a positive general mental attitude. If you miss a shot, don't blame your racket, the sun, the court, the moon—you did it. Big deal. That means you can also correct it. However, if you miss a shot, blame your racket, and go on to the next point, you haven't learned or gained anything, because who knows when your racket is going to start behaving itself?

Often, in our desire to see and do only good, we tend not to admit our failures. Not that long ago in my tennis career I came to realize that I had been putting on blinders to avoid seeing a certain aspect of my game. All players "choke" to some degree; that is, they get overly tense at critical moments in a match and make bad errors. However, no one likes to admit to other people or themselves that they choke. I made both those mistakes, but by not admitting to myself during a match that I was choking was the most damaging error, because then I couldn't deal with it. During a match in which I was choking, I would start missing my first serve, which prevented me from following my serve up to the net, where I was comfortable. Denying to myself that I was choking, I would then try to hit my first serve harder than ever, generally missing even more. The ridiculously simple solution to my problem was made very clear to me by a conversation I had one day with Billie Jean. In describing a tense moment in a match of hers she said, "I was choking out of my gourd, so I knew I better get my first serve in and get my bahoola up to net. So I took a little off my first serve and just spun it in deep to make sure I got it in. When I'm choking I always

146

know to aim a little deeper than normal because, when I'm tense, I have a tendency to hit short."

This conversation with Billie Jean hammered home two points for me. First, even the greatest players can choke, so why should I be embarrassed when I do? Maybe that's what makes the great players great—they more readily admit their mistakes. Second, by realizing at the time that she was choking and admitting it, she could deal with it and devise a game plan to compensate for her deficiencies. In this way Billie Jean used the negative feedback available to her (first service errors and tenseness) to attain a positive result (getting her first serve in). As Dr. Maxwell Maltz says in his book *Psycho-Cybernetics,* "The first step toward becoming stronger is the recognition that you are weak."

5. *Forget your mistakes.* Once you have taken note of your mistakes, forget them. Don't dwell on them or else they can creep up and inadvertently become the images held in your mind as end results. Let's say you are playing a set and reach a terrific point where both you and your opponent are scrambling all over the court making fine shots. Finally, you get into a position to make a winning shot and you blow it and thump the ball into the net. In reality you have made ten excellent shots and just one mistake. If tennis were scored differently, it might be 10–1 for you. However, because of the way tennis is scored, the only shot you think of and remember is the last one you missed. You can't seem to shake it, and keep reliving the moment in your mind, all the while berating yourself for your lack of coordination and stupidity. What you are effectively doing is feeding your computer negative feedback. You need both positive and negative feedback for maximum learning benefit. Feed your computer only negative data and the results will be negative.

6. *Relax and trust your computer.* There is nothing more natural or automatic than breathing. If you focus on your breathing, suddenly it doesn't seem as easy or nat-

ural; it's almost a little bit like work. You feel less relaxed. A tennis stroke is not an automatic function like breathing, but it reacts the same way to overattention. Worry about your forehand, analyze it too much, and suddenly it becomes even more difficult to perform. After you have learned the basic tennis skills and have prepared to the best of your ability, you have to relax and let it happen. Trust your computer to make it happen. Tennis strokes aren't arbitrary movements but have evolved because of their biomechanical efficiency and compatibility with the human body. Your arm *wants* to swing in a naturally correct manner; only over-thinking, tension, and distrust will prevent it. A note of warning: this advice is not a license to be lazy. Through hard work, practice, and careful preparation you feed your computer with the necessary bits of information to produce the desired end result. There is nothing more relaxing or trust inducing than knowing you have prepared totally and are 100 percent ready.

Coping with Pressure

Pressure can bring out the best or the worst in people. Some people buckle under the first hint of stress whereas others raise themselves to new heights of achievement. Fortunately, people aren't born with an ability or inability to cope with pressure, but acquire it through life. Since pressure physical and mental, is an intrinsic part of sports, a child can start learning positive ways of dealing with pressure through tennis.

Here are some suggestions to help a child deal with stress on the court.

1. *Practice without pressure.* To illustrate this point, let us again refer to Dr. Maltz's book.

Not long ago I visited a friend of mine one Sunday in a suburb of New York. His ten-year-old son had visions of becoming a big-league baseball star. His fielding was adequate, but he couldn't hit. Each time his father threw the ball across the plate, the boy froze up—and missed it a foot. I decided to try something. "You're so anxious to hit the ball, and so afraid you won't, that you can't even see it clearly," I said. All that tension and anxiety was interfering with his eyesight and his reflexes—his arm muscles weren't executing the orders from his brain.

"For the next ten pitches," I said, "don't even try to hit the ball. Don't try at all. Keep your bat on your shoulder. But watch the ball *very* carefully. Keep your eyes on it from the time it leaves your Daddy's hand until it goes by you. Stand easy and loose, and just watch the ball go by."

After ten trials of this, I advised him, "Now, for a while, watch the ball go by and keep the bat on your shoulder, but think to yourself you are going to bring the bat around so it will really hit the ball—solidly and dead-center." After this, I told him to keep on "feeling the same way" and to keep watching the ball carefully, and to "let" the bat come around and meet the ball, making no attempt to hit it hard. The boy hit the ball. After a few easy hits like this, he was knocking the ball a country mile, and I had a friend for life.

The maximum amount of learning occurs when a person is in a relaxed yet alert state. Thus, for players to gain the most out of practice, it should be done without pressure.

2. *Use sleep to imagine the best.* Go to sleep with success images on your mind. Just before falling asleep, be extremely relaxed and receptive to new "computer data." How often have you daydreamed about something nice happening, and lo and behold, it happened! There is nothing magical or mystical in this occurrence. What you have unconsciously done is given your computer specific, desired end results to aim for. And because you

weren't consciously trying to achieve these results, you were relaxed and let your computer achieve your goals without the obstacles of tension or overthinking. So, let your dreams help you accomplish your goals.

3. *Don't confuse excitement with fear.* Physiologically, the body's reactions to excitement and fear are identical. It is only a person's mental state that determines whether the whole emotional response is labeled "excitement" or "fear." Thus, two people may be sitting in a room waiting to play a tournament match. One person looks at her sweaty palms, feels her heart thumping and her stomach jumping, and thinks "Oh boy, am I scared! How am I ever going to go out and play?" The other player notices the same physical manifestations, but thinks, "Oh boy, am I ready! Let me out there!" The first girl has chosen to be scared, the second to be excited. Be aware that you can make these choices for yourself. Everyone gets nervous and even scared, but don't let the physical signs of nervousness make you more scared and too tense to react adequately. Accept them as natural, and even as a positive, as a sign that your body is primed for action.

4. *Concentrate on what you are going to do, not on what your opponent is going to do.* Realize that you can only control those happenings that are within your power to control, and your opponent is not one of them. Don't be so preoccupied with what your opponent is going to do that you forget to watch the ball or move your feet. Stay focused on the here and now and on the end results that you want. Let your opponent worry about himself.

5. *Imagine the worst.* If you're really tied up and feeling overwhelmed by pressure, try imagining the very worst that can happen. In a tennis match the worst that can happen is that you will lose. So what—one of you must, and there's always another match. Usually, if you imagine the worst, you realize things aren't quite so bad, not quite so life and death. Pretty soon you'll find that

150

you're more relaxed and better prepared to perform the necessary tasks.

6. *Remember to breathe.* This suggestion may sound silly, but often during strenuous exercise at stressful moments, people forget to breathe—just when they need it the most, too. In psychotherapy, during very emotional moments, it's quite common for the client to start holding his breath, and breathe very irregularly. Breathing in this way leads to a noticeable increase in tension. In these cases, I generally stop the discussion and have the client focus on breathing deeply and regularly to induce relaxation, so that the emotionally loaded topic can be tackled more calmly.

This same process is extremely helpful in tennis, where a player needs not only to relax but must have all the oxygen he can possibly get. Deep breathing was used quite effectively by Arthur Ashe at Wimbledon in 1974 on his way to winning the championship. During his matches on the changeovers, Arthur would sit in his seat, close his eyes, and take a number of deep breaths. Whatever else he was doing or thinking, he was breathing deeply, giving his body much oxygen and relaxing his mind and body to go back out ready and refreshed. So to help bring about relaxation at critical times, before a point or during the court changeover, concentrate on breathing deeply and regularly.

We've now covered some of the mental aspects of the game that are most important, some of which are far easier talked about than done. I know, however, that they work, and they not only work in tennis but in life, so one should never stop trying to use them. Sports are said to be character building, but no one makes it quite clear exactly how an athlete's character gets built. If the suggestions here are followed, they will not only help your child build character in tennis, but in life. In larger terms, we've actually been talking about honesty with oneself and others, self-acceptance (both the good and bad), developing a positive outlook on life, coping with pressure, and being able to concenorate under sure.

Stroke Reminders

As important as the mental aspects of tennis are, they cannot be used to the maximum benefit unless a child has good, solid technique. A brief walk around the grounds of the U.S. Open at Flushing Meadow will make the point clearly that all the best players in the world don't hit the ball identically. Each player has his own idiosyncratic way of hitting the ball. There are, however, certain commonalities that all the good players share, which we will point out in this section. This is not an instruction section—we leave that to a child's coach—but a section that will, we hope, remind children of some elements taught by their coaches.

Throughout his years of teaching, Nick has found the adage "less is more" to be very true in tennis. Give a student too much to think about, and watch his game deteriorate. However, give that same student one or two things to concentrate on, and watch everything else fall into place. Below are some pointers that should reinforce what a child has already been taught. They are sketchy on purpose, in order to avoid contradicting a child's coach.

Ready position (Figure 11)

1. Watch the ball!
2. Feet shoulder-width apart.
3. Weight forward, knees slightly bent, body relaxed.
4. Racket-head shoulder height.
5. Elbows slightly away from body.

Figure 11.

Figure 12A.

Figure 12B.

Forehand

1. Watch the ball!
2. Prepare quickly with a shoulder turn.
3. Lay the wrist back slightly on backswing.
4. Firm wrist on contact.
5. Close the racket face slightly on backswing for topspin.

Figure 12C.

Figure 12D.

6. When making contact with the ball, step toward the net, not across.
7. Meet the ball out in front of the body (toward the net).
8. Finish with the racket above the opposite shoulder. (Low to high swing on forward part of stroke for topspin).
9. Short backswing with a long follow-through.

Figure 13A.

Figure 13B.

Backhand

1. Watch the ball!
2. Prepare quickly with a shoulder turn.
3. Use the left hand for support on the throat of the racket on the backswing.
4. Let the racket, arm, and shoulder turn as a unit when starting the forward swing.

Figure 13C.

Figure 13D.

5. Get the racket head below the ball on the forward swing.
6. Swing from low to high for topspin.
7. Meet the ball out in front of the body.
8. Step forward, not across, to hit the ball.
9. Keep the wrist firm during the entire swing.
10. Keep the arm and racket fairly close to the body on the backswing.

Figure 14A.

Figure 14B.

11. When hitting a two-handed backhand, have both arms and hands moving together. Neither arm is dominant.

Figure 14C.

Figure 14D.

Figure 15A.

Figure 15B.

Volley

1. Watch the ball!
2. Wrist firm at all times.
3. Short backswing.
4. Short follow-through.
5. Volley out, not down.

Figure 15C.

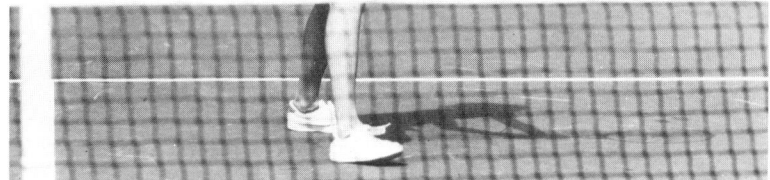

Figure 15D.

6. On low volleys, bend the knees and get down to the level of the ball.
7. Turn shoulders slightly.
8. First volley is for position and depth, not to be hit as a winner.
9. Move in closer for the second volley.

Figure 16A.   Figure 16B.

Serve

1. Watch the ball!
2. Arm and wrist to be loose and relaxed at all times.
3. Ball arm and racket arm should go down together and up together (on opposite sides of the body) to develop a rhythm.
4. Limit unnecessary body motions.

162

Figure 16C.   Figure 16D.

5. The ball should be released from the full extended arm and fingertips.
6. The ball should be thrown to a position slightly in front and to the right of the left foot (for righthanders).
7. Arm and racket should reach up to make contact with the ball at the highest point.
8. Keep chin up and watch racket make contact with the ball.

Figure 17A.

Figure 17B.

Overhead

1. Watch the ball!
2. Turn to the side, then move to the ball.
3. Get the racket up and ready while moving.

ₒure 17C.   Figure 17D.

4. Keep the chin up.
5. Point to the ball with the opposite hand.
6. Reach up for the ball and make contact with it slightly in front of you.

There is so much more to talk about regarding stroke production, but we're not writing an instruction manual. Instead, we have just offered some reminders that a child might think about while drifting off to sleep, and pick one or two of them to work on while playing.

WE HEAR HOW sports are 75 percent mental and 25 percent physical, but we aren't really given many specifics regarding the mental side of athletics. In what ways are sports "mental"? How can one improve one's "mental game"? In this chapter we have included coaching tips for both the mental side of a child's game and the physical one. Both sides entail learned behavior that can be modified and improved. We hope that a child, while learning a healthful life-long sport, will also learn healthful and enduring ways of dealing with his environment mentally and emotionally.

9.

Practice

Here comes the typical twosome out for some tennis practice. They go out on the tennis court and start rallying. The ball bounces once, twice, three times, four times; it bounces so darn long you can play marbles by the time the other player finally hits it. Player A hits to Player B who hits right back to A. A hits a ball five feet from B. "Sorry! Didn't mean to hit it there." No one moves. "Boy! We're hitting well today. Nothing like getting some exercise!" That's how most people practice, and that's why most people don't improve. Nick calls this kind of practice a total waste of time, saying, "The advice that I can give to all players, regardless of their ability, is always to have a practice plan whenever they go out to play."

In this chapter we will discuss why, how, and with whom a child should practice. Various specific drills will be described that players of all levels can do that are fun as well as helpful tools in improving one's game.

Before we discuss why someone should practice, let's make it perfectly clear exactly what practice is. Practice occurs when a player chooses a particular segment of his game to concentrate on and work on repeatedly, perhaps at the temporary expense of other aspects. Thus, practice is definitely not hitting the ball back and forth aimlessly, even if hours and hours are spent doing it. Thirty minutes of organized practice is worth more than four hours of sloppy, nonfocused hitting. Practice is also not going out and playing games and sets with the sole object of winning. Under competitive circumstances, it's only natural to want to win. Therefore, one has a tendency to practice one's strengths, not weaknesses. Games and sets can be played for practice if

167

the player has the mental attitude that he is working on a technique or strategy and winning is secondary.

Why?

There are various reasons why a player should practice, but we feel the most important is to have fun. This might sound a little like trying to convince a young pianist that playing scales is a barrel of laughs (although, luckily, tennis practice can be made much more fun than piano scales, as we will discuss later). Let us explain. Because tennis is such a complex game, demanding a good deal of skill, it's almost impossible even to stay the same without practice. The game is not like riding a bicycle, which once you have the knack you always have. A tennis game left unattended deteriorates; with a minimum of practice, it stays the same; and with even more practice, it improves.

We believe that playing good tennis and making noticeable improvements is the most fun a player can have. However, these pleasures aren't free and are attained only by paying a certain price, which is practice. So, rather than suffer the disappointments of regressing or standing still, we feel a player has much more fun making short-term sacrifices in order to reap long-term gains. This philosophy has to be explained carefully to children, since they have a strong impulse toward instant gratification. Children are, however, extremely good at working toward long-term goals, as long as they are able to achieve many short-term goals along the way.

Practice itself can be fun, because only then can a player experience true competition-free, pressureless tennis. Yes, practice can be tedious and even a bit arduous, but the sense of accomplishment after such sessions is well worth it all. Besides, practice need not be boring. With a little imagination and organization, practice sessions can be filled with drill games that are not only fun but productive.

For the more serious player, practice is necessary, to "overlearn." By overlearning we mean that a player will try to learn a part of the game so well as to make it almost automatic, so that in a pressure-filled match situation he will be able to perform adequately. Overlearning can apply even to physical strength. In my tournament experience, I've found that because of the addition of nerves and stress to a match, three hours of practice tennis is physically equivalent to only about one hour of tournament tennis. When I'm in training I know that I have to practice four, five, and sometimes six hours a day in order to build up the physical endurance sufficient for a two- or three-hour match.

How Much?

No one can say how much someone must practice, because we are all different and have unique abilities and needs. Some children's attention spans are very short, and they should only practice a short time, but with good concentration. Other children will want to stay out there until they are dragged in. The important thing is the quality of practice, not the quantity. As a rough estimate, we would say that without a minimum of about six hours a week on the court, it would be hard for a child to improve.

How to Practice

Even some tournament pros don't know how to practice properly. When I was growing up, coaching was not as intense, organized, or thorough as it is today, and no one really taught me how to practice. My practice consisted of going out, hitting a little of this, a little of that, playing a set or two, and hoping I'd get better. It wasn't until 1974, when I played for the Philadelphia Freedoms and had Billie Jean King as my coach, that I learned what practice was all about. Listed below are the basic practice methods I use constantly for my game and that Nick has for his students.

1. *Have a definite plan.* Each time you go out to play, know exactly what you're going to work on. If you've been

missing a lot of volleys, decide to spend some time on those. Talk to your coach and have him suggest a practice plan. Maybe your footwork needs to be improved or your reflexes quickened. You may want to do crosscourt backhand drills and then play a set, trying to incorporate as many crosscourt backhands as possible. Whatever you do, be specific and know what you want to get done in that practice session.

2. *Practice intensely.* Give 110 percent when you practice. You may not last as long as you can when you're less intense, but the rewards will be far greater. Try for every ball, whether you think you can reach it or not. Many times you'll surprise yourself by hitting some balls you didn't think you could reach. When I practice, one of my goals is always to at least touch the ball, even if I don't think I can hit it. When Rod Laver practices, he tries for every ball inside or outside the court. If he can't reach it on the first bounce, he keeps running hard until he does reach it and hit it back. He feels that by making this supreme effort, balls that bounce inside the court in matches will seem relatively easy.

3. *Take frequent breaks.* In psychology it is known that more learning takes place with distributed practices than with massed practices. In other words, a player will benefit more from practicing 30 minutes, taking a 10-minute break, and practicing another 30 minutes than from practicing for 60 minutes straight. In order to practice intensely, you must take frequent time-outs to refresh both mind and body.

4. *Practice both weak and strong points.* Many players make the mistake of practicing only their best shots. That's fine, as long as you have an agreement with your opponents not to hit to your weak areas. Remember, making mistakes is part of the learning process; if you don't make them, you won't improve. Be stubborn and decide to turn your weaknesses into strengths, and the only way you're going to do that is by hitting thousands of balls with your weak shots.

Another mistake players can make is to concentrate so hard on improving weaknesses that they forget to practice their strengths. Recently, Martina Navratilova was working extremely hard on improving her backhand. She never gave a second thought to her forehand (probably the best in women's tennis), because she felt so sure of it. Suddenly, the tables were turned and she found herself making more forehand errors than backhand ones, because she had forgotten to practice her forehand. Always practice all your shots, but spend a little more time on your weaknesses.

5. *Practice mentally and physically.* Whenever you're on the court, practice the mental coaching tips discussed in Chapter 8. Remember to have both short-term and long-term goals in mind. Visualize an end result for each shot. Concentrate on one thing at a time. Don't be afraid to make mistakes; learn from them and then forget them. Instruct yourself in positives, not negatives.

6. *Change routines frequently.* Practice is as fun or as boring as you make it. Later we suggest a number of drills you can use, but there are many more that can be created. Invent your own drills that fit your particular needs. Be imaginative. Within any one practice session, change your drills often. You're not going to perfect your strokes in one session, so don't beat a drill to death. Keeping fresh and keeping your motivation high is the most important factor, so keep a lot of variety in your practice sessions.

Practice Partners

A child should practice with a variety of practice partners— better, worse, and equal to him in ability. Against a player of lesser ability a child can gain confidence by being able consistently to win practice matches. A child can be on the offensive, push his opponent around, be more willing to practice weaknesses, and experiment with new shots. Against an opponent of equal stature, a child will have to concentrate harder and be more analytical of his game. Being fairly evenly matched with an opponent gives a player a good opportunity to pinpoint exactly where he is getting beaten. To beat an opponent of equal ability generally requires cutting down on unforced errors. If both players are evenly matched on strengths, the one who commits the fewest mistakes will win. Against a better player, a child will be forced to squeeze that little extra out of his game. Not only will he have to play well and commit few errors, but he must also learn to jump on any opportunities and make the most of them. Better players only allow an opponent a few chances to get a foot in the door. A child has to learn to recognize these opportunities and take advantage of them.

A child should be grouped with players he can beat *and* be beaten by. It is just as important to learn from superior players as it is to gain confidence by playing people you can beat. It also helps to play older children, because that takes some of the pressure off winning.

Along with opponents of varying abilities, a child should try to practice with opponents of widely varying styles. The greater overall variety a child can have in practice sessions, the more flexible and adaptable to new situations he will be.

Practice Drills

The number of practice drills is virtually endless. One very good book devoted entirely to drills is *Tennis Drills* by Robert Ford Greene (see Suggestions for Further Reading for details). The following are some of the drills Nick (in his teaching) and I (in my practicing) use regularly. A general rule to follow when doing these drills is always to work on accuracy and consistency first, then on pace. Also, always set either time or shot goals to be met by each drill. For example, do a drill for five minutes or until twenty consecutive good shots have been hit.

Two-Player Drills

These drills assume both players are right-handed, but drills can be altered to accommodate left-handers.

1. *Crosscourt groundstroke drill*   Players stand behind the baseline (see Figure 18 for court labels) and rally either forehand to forehand or backhand to backhand.

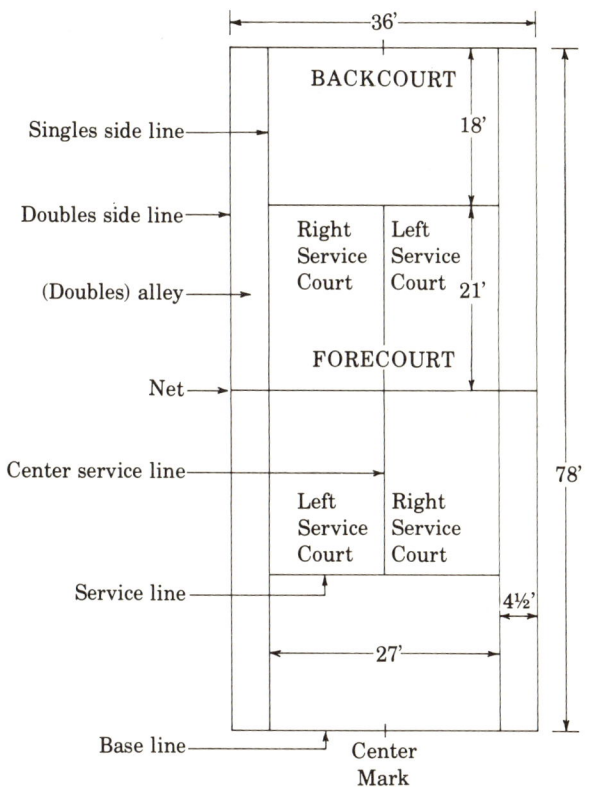

Figure 18. The Tennis Court.

After each hit, players should try to go back to the ready position at the center of the court behind the baseline in order to simulate gamelike footwork. The target areas are generally either deep in the corner or near the junction of the side and service lines for the short-angle shot. All balls should be played, whether inside or outside the court. Racket covers or towels may be placed on the court as targets. Players should hit with little pace at first, striving only for accuracy and consistency. Pace can be picked up as players become more adept at the drill. Set either time or shot goals. For instance, go on to the next drill after twenty consecutive "good" shots (those landing between service and baselines to correct corners) have been hit or 10 minutes have elapsed. You can even play a game by scoring every time a target has been hit.

2. *Down-the-line groundstrokes*   From their baselines the two players rally, one stroking forehands, the other stroking backhands, thus sending the ball on a path parallel to the sideline. The ideal target area is two to four feet from the sideline and two to four feet from the baseline. Set shot or time goals. Again, targets can be placed and a game played by hitting the targets. If targets aren't being hit regularly, make them bigger, and gradually decrease their size when accuracy increases.

3. *One-hundred-ball drill*   Players rally from the baseline, counting as good only those shots landing in the court between the service line and baseline. One hundred consecutive good shots must be hit. The counting starts again after a "bad" shot. This drill teaches sustained concentration and patience, which are particularly useful on slow surfaces like clay.

4. *Depth and height drill*   A line approximately five feet within the baseline and parallel to it is drawn with chalk, string, rope, towels, or whatever. Players, rallying from their baselines, aim for the area between the drawn line and the baseline. Since depth is most easily achieved by increasing height over the net, the players

174

are urged to concentrate on clearing the net by at least five feet, as well as aiming for the target area.

5. *Follow-the-leader drill* One player is the designated leader, the other the follower. The follower must hit whatever shot the leader hits. Roles are switched after an allotted amount of time. This drill encourages the use of variety within one rally and use of the whole court.

6. *Crosscourt and down-the-line drill* Rallying from the baselines, one player hits only crosscourt shots while the other hits only down-the-line shots. This drill entails quite a bit of running from side to side and is therefore excellent in developing accuracy and consistency while on the run. It also clearly teaches an important strategic lesson—the player hitting down the line must run faster and be ready to hit sooner than the crosscourt hitter, because down-the-line shots travel a shorter distance and take less time to get to the other side. Thus, if a player needs to buy extra time to get back into position, he should always hit for the longest distance, which is crosscourt.

7. *Crosscourt volley drill* One player is up at net in the volleying position and the other is at the baseline. Players hit forehand or backhand to backhand. The target area for the volleyer is ideally deep to the crosscourt corner and at least beyond the service line. This drill is good for developing depth in volleys and hitting the ball early.

8. *Down-the-line volley drill* With one player at net and the other at the baseline, players hit forehand to backhand, sending the ball in a path parallel to the sideline. The target area for the volleyer should be at least beyond the service line and ideally in the corner. This drill is good for teaching the players to get in a sideways hitting position, since down-the-line shots are most easily hit when standing completely sideways to the net.

9. *Half-court drill* Using only half the court, including the doubles alleys, one player stands at net and the

other at the baseline, both midway between the center line and doubles sideline. The players can either use the same halves (e.g., each player's backhand side of the court) for crosscourt rallies or opposite halves for down-the-line rallies. A game is played to five points, in which the baseline player tries to score with passing shots and lobs, and the volleyer tries to score with volley and overhead smash placements. Either player can begin the rally, and scoring begins after the ball has crossed the net three consecutive times. Players should switch net and baseline positions and court halves after each game so that all possible crosscourt and down-the-line combinations have been played. This drill is good for groundstroke passing shots and lobs, volleys, and smashes, and for footwork.

10. *Quick volley drill* Both players stand just inside the service line and volley back and forth. Pace should be increased as quickly as possible. Five-point games can be played. For more advanced players, a variation on the drill is to have each player try to advance one step closer to the net with each volley. This drill is excellent for quickening reflexes and footwork.

11. *Up-and-back drill* With one player at net and the other at the baseline, the player at the baseline alternately hits lobs and ground strokes. Thus, the player at net is alternately hitting overheads and volleys. The volleyer should pay careful attention to moving forward to get back to the proper net position after hitting an overhead. This drill can also be done with the baseline player standing in one corner or the other, so the volleyer must smash and volley to a more confined area. It is excellent stamina work for the volleyer, as well as good practice for volleys, overheads, and footwork. For the baseliner, this still provides good practice for hitting ground strokes off smashes and for lobbing.

12. *Short-court drill* Both players stand just behind their service line and rally. Score may be kept and a ten-point game played. This drill is primarily used to develop fi-

nesse and touch since slices, short angles, and drop shots are most commonly used.

13. *Serve and service return drill* One player serves and the other returns serve. Targets such as tennis cans, racket covers, or towels are placed for both players. A game can be played where points are scored for hitting the targets. The server should practice both first and second serves. The target areas for the server's first serve are in both corners and about five feet from the service line toward the net along the sideline for short angle serves. Target areas for the second serve are not quite as close to the lines (although depth is still important) and are, therefore, about three feet in from the sideline toward the center line and two to four feet inside the service line. The target areas for the returner are more numerous, but two common ones are in the down-the-line and crosscourt corners.

Often a child may find himself part of an odd trio on the court instead of in a twosome or foursome. Not to worry—there are excellent drills for three people on a court called two-on-one drills. In fact, these drills are preferred by many touring pros because they come closer to matchlike situations and provide a strenuous physical workout. The beauty of two-on-one drills is that the player can work on both stroke production and physical stamina. The general form of the drills is as follows: Two players are on one side against one on the other. The focus of the drill is always on the "one," who is allowed to hit full out and go for winning shots. The "two" work on their control and try to feed shots to the "one" that are within the "one's" reach, but for which he must scramble. The "one" is obligated to try for each shot. This drill lasts only five or ten minutes before the players rotate positions to give the "one" a much needed rest. A supply of at least twenty balls is necessary to keep these drills going smoothly, because whenever the "one" misses a shot, one of the "two" always has a ball in the hand to hit immediately, to keep the "one" running. Other two-on-one drills are:

1. *Ground stroke two-on-one drill* The "one" is at the baseline and the "two" are at net. The "one" practices any variety of shots, using more pace than he would ordinarily use, and tries to pass and occasionally lob over the "two." The "two" keep the ball in play and force the "one" to run from side to side and up and back.
2. *Volley two-on-one drill* The "one" is at net and the "two" are at the baseline. The "two" move the "one" from side to side, back with lobs, and forward again with ground strokes. The "one" tries to put the ball away and hit all shots before they bounce. If a lob gets over the "one's" head, he must run back and try to retrieve it. By the way, other names for these exercises are "suicide" and "kamikaze" drills.

Backboard Drills

A child need never be at loss for practice if a partner can't be found, because there are several specific drills that can be done against a backboard, garage door, or wall.

1. *Target practice* Tape pieces of paper for targets to the backboard, or draw targets with chalk. Aim for the targets, counting how many times you hit them in a rally. Practice ground strokes, volleys, and serves this way.
2. *Consistency drills* Estimate the height of the net (three feet) and draw a "net" line on the backboard. Hitting ground strokes, count how many consecutive good shots (above the net) you can hit. Peaches Bartkowicz, the Tracy Austin of my junior days, and known as the "human backboard," was feared for her incredibly steady ground strokes. She just never made unforced errors. She and her coach, Mrs. Jean Hoxie of Hamtramck, Michigan, attributed her extraordinary consistency to all the hours she put in with a backboard. Mrs. Hoxie would have Peaches hit against a backboard every day for at least an hour. In fact, at one point when Peaches was just seven years old, she held the record for

the most consecutive good shots against a backboard, which was well over a thousand!

This drill can also be done with volleys and is excellent for strengthening the arm muscles.

3. *Reflex drills* By hitting the ball harder or stepping closer to the board, you can make the ball come back faster, forcing you to prepare earlier. By moving closer to the board on volleys, you can simulate the quick volley drill described before. Also, a good way to work on footwork for ground strokes and volleys is to alternate hitting forehands and backhands. This forces you to take quick, small steps to get in the sideways hitting position.

Group Drills

If you have a group of players, a large quantity of balls, and take turns having one person be the "feeder," a number of excellent drills can be done. These drills, designed to simulate game action movements, allow the players to practice shots repeatedly, in order to make them automatic. They are also designed to improve footwork and balance. Safety procedures should be followed by keeping the court cleared of balls and the players spaced well apart to avoid accidents. After a player's turn, he should help clear balls and then return to the back of the line (or to the other line if there are two) for another turn.

1. *Windshield Wiper Volley Drill*
   a) Feeder X stands behind the service line with the balls. Net player A stands about 8 feet from the net on the center line, while net player B stands at the net on the singles sideline. Players C and D stand about 7 feet behind A and B respectively. See Figure 19.
   b) First X hits the ball wide to A's left so that he moves over to hit a backhand volley (a). At the same time, B slides across to the center line and "shadow hits" a backhand volley. At the time A is making contact with the

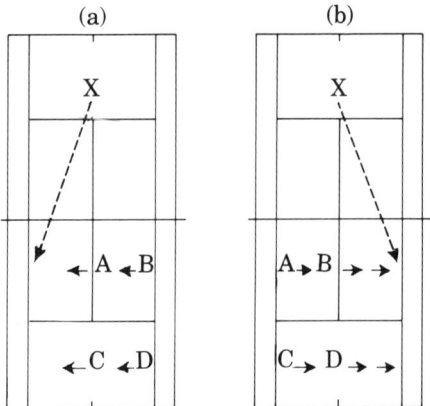

(a)   (b)

Figure 19. Windshield Wiper Volley Drill.

backhand volley, X hits a ball wide to B's right, forcing him to recover and hit a forehand volley (b). As B is moving toward the forehand volley, A is sliding toward the center line, "shadowing" a forehand volley. The two volleyers move as if they are tied together. Hence the "windshield wiper" action.

c) Now C and D move at the same time as A and B and shadow their movements.

d) The exercise is repeated for several shots.

2. *Windshield Wiper Baseline Drill*
This drill is an adaptation of the Windshield Wiper Volley Drill. The only change is that the hitters (A and B) line up at the baseline and hit ground strokes instead of volleys.

3. *Windshield Wiper Ground Stroke and Volley Drill*
a) Feeder X stands behind the service line with the balls. Net player B stands 8 feet from the net and on the center line. Baseliner A stands in the center of the court on the baseline. See Figure 20.

180

(a) (b) (c)

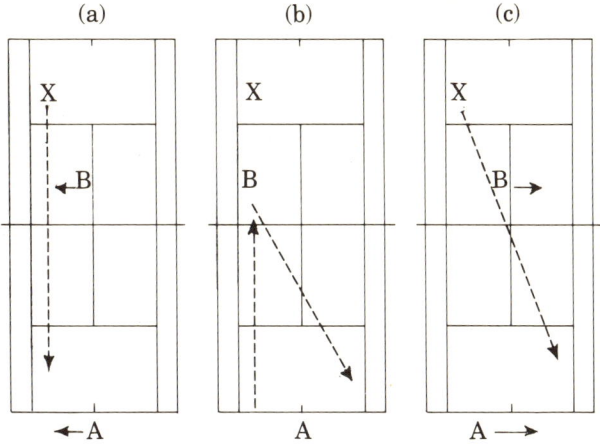

Figure 20. Windshield Wiper Ground Stroke and Volley Drill.

b) First X hits the ball down the line. Then A moves to return the backhand down the line while B slides toward the same line to cut off the return with a crosscourt volley (a and b).

c) Then X hits a ball crosscourt. Now A moves to return the ball down the line while B slides across to cut off the shot with a crosscourt volley (c).

d) The exercise is repeated for several shots.

4. *Four-ball Drill.* See Figure 21.

a) Feeder X stands on the baseline with the balls. Hitter A lines up at the center of the baseline. Now X hits the first ball deep to A's forehand. Then A returns the ball to X's backhand corner with depth (a).

b) Next, X hits the second ball shallow to A, who takes this ball as an approach shot and hits it down the line (b).

c) Completing the approach shot, A moves in to take a first volley. A hits it crosscourt, deep, but not for a winner (c).

181

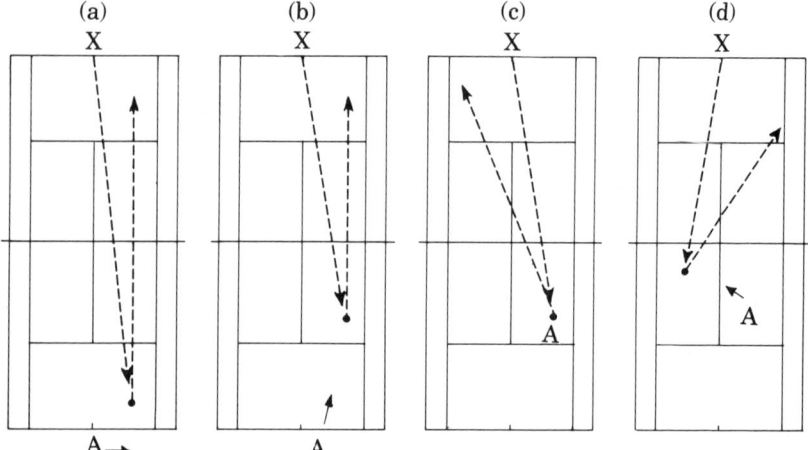

Figure 21. Four-ball Drill.

d) Then A closes in toward the net to put away the second volley (d).

Drills to Help You Watch the Ball

These drills can be done while doing other drills or by themselves.

1. *Bounce-hit drill* This drill was developed by W. Timothy Gallwey, the author of *Inner Tennis*. While rallying, the player says "hit" when he hits the ball, "bounce" when the ball bounces on his opponent's side, "hit" when the ball bounces back on his side, and so forth. Players who do not really watch the ball the whole way will find that their vocalization of "hit" or "bounce" will not synchronize with the event. Thus, to do this drill properly, the player must focus his full attention on watching the ball. This drill is excellent for players of all levels, from beginners to pros. It is also particularly good when a

182

player changes court surfaces and has to readjust the timing of his strokes.

2. *Analyzing the ball* While rallying or serving, the player should try to focus on some aspect of the ball. For example, he should try to read the brand name on the ball, see the seams, or notice the direction of the spin. The player can get so involved in analyzing the ball that watching it for the full flight becomes automatic and effortless.

Drills for Young Children or Recent Beginners

Before some very young players or beginners can produce a stroke and make contact with the ball, they have to acquaint themselves with the racket and get a feel for the distance between their hand and the racket head. These drills are designed to help these players develop eye–racket coordination, as opposed to eye—hand coordination.

1. *Bouncing the ball* On any surface where a tennis ball can bounce, the player, holding the racket by the handle with any grip, bounces the ball on the ground with the racket. The child can count how many times he can do it without missing.

2. *Bouncing the ball in the air* After the child can bounce the ball on the ground fairly well, he can now try hitting it straight up into the air. Again, the child can play a game by counting the number of consecutive hits before a miss. The child can vary this and the preceding drill by alternating the sides of the racket face for each hit, or by imparting spin on the ball instead of hitting it flatly.

PRACTICE IS going to make the difference in both a child's tennis game and his enjoyment of the game. Without a minimum amount of practice a child will not improve and will become discouraged and bored with the game. Practice in itself can be fun and challenging, and if done efficiently need not take a great deal of time.

10.

Sportsmanship

As do all other sports, tennis has its own official rules. (The written rules, obtained by writing the U.S. Tennis Association, 30 East 42nd Street, New York, New York 10017, should be read and learned thoroughly by all players, particularly players who intend to play in school, club, or tournament matches.) Unlike other sports, in tennis not every important match is presided over by officials, leaving the burden of officiating to the players. In a school basketball game, coaches, assistants, and officials would be there to enforce the rules, keep the score, and record the winner. The players would not even have to know the rules, since officials would be there to implement all the rules and preside over any disagreements. On the other hand, if a child has a school tennis match, he would report to the main tennis desk, meet his opponent, be given three balls, sent to a certain court, and be told that the winner should come back with the scores and balls. It would be up to him and his opponent to know the rules, abide by them, and also know and abide by the unwritten rules of good conduct and court etiquette. Thus, it's obvious that in tennis a great deal of responsibility is put on a child's personal honor system. This chapter deals with those written and unwritten rules of honor and etiquette, how they can be violated and why, and how a child can cope with players who do violate them.

The Player's Code

For those readers who aren't familiar with tennis, it may not be apparent why there is a need for a player's code, or

184

how the official rules can be abused in fact and in spirit. The following is an incident that will illustrate the ambiguities that exist in tennis. Years ago I was playing a junior tournament match where we had no official on court. Therefore, the line calls and scorekeeping were the responsibility of me and my opponent. During one rally my opponent hit a shot that got by me and hit very near the line. I didn't get a really good look at it and, adhering to the first rule of tennis etiquette (that you must call a ball good unless you clearly see it out), I called the ball good. Later on in the match a similar event occurred, only this time it was I who hit the shot and my opponent who was making the call. My opponent, obviously in a quandary as to how to call the ball, looked up and said, "I can't tell how it was. Let's play a let." I doubt if my opponent was trying to cheat, but the fact is that in tennis you do not play a point over unless a player has hit a let serve or there has been interference in the play. Thus, in order not to be, or appear to be, anything but totally honest, it is important that a child know the player's code and use it in all unofficiated games, practices, and tournaments. Below are the major provisions of the code, which is available through the U.S. Tennis Association.

1. In making a line call, unless you clearly see the ball out, you must call it good. Thus, doubt is always resolved in favor of your opponent. No lets should be played, and the ball should certainly not be called out if there is any doubt. "When in doubt, call out" is purely for cheaters.
2. In an unofficiated game, only you and your opponent are responsible for line calls—no one else. Thus, do not ask spectators for advice on a line call. Even if they were paying attention, they were probably in no position to see the shot with an accurate perspective. However, you may ask your opponent for an opinion, because in some cases he or she may have had a better view of the shot than you.
3. If you *clearly* see one of your shots out on your opponent's side, you are obligated to call it.

4. Calls of "out" or "let" should be made instantaneously in order to avoid the "two-chance" option that some players try to practice. The two-chance option is illustrated by this example. During a match I hit a good first serve, followed it to net, and volleyed away a winner. After the point was finished, my opponent said, "I think I heard a let. Play two." That type of behavior led me to wonder if my opponent would have called a let had she won the point. Essentially, my opponent had given herself two chances to win that point.
5. A player must allow a ball to bounce before calling it out. If a ball is hit, hits the player, or is caught by the player before it bounces, it is presumed to be good.
6. In doubles, if one partner calls the ball good and the other partner calls it out, the doubt that is established means the ball must be called good.
7. It is considered rude for a receiver to return a serve that is obviously out (accompanied by an out call). If it is known that this is disturbing to the server, then it is gamesmanship—a subtle form of cheating. In officiated tournament matches, players may return close out serves, thereby putting to use the policy that all balls are good unless called out by the official. In this case the intention is to play according to the official's line calls, not to disturb the opponent.
8. Foot faulting is against the official rules, but unfortunately impossible for a receiver to call in an unofficiated match. Thus, it is up to each player's personal honor system to make sure he is not foot faulting. As Tony Trabert says, "You don't let the ball bounce twice before you hit it and expect your opponent to let you get away with it, do you? No, because it's against the rules. Well, why do you think foot faulting is okay? It's breaking a rule, too. You can't obey some rules and ignore others."
9. Players should not talk aloud or act in any way to disturb their opponents or players on neighboring courts.

Thus, if you make an exclamation while the ball is in play, your opponent is entitled to a let, provided he makes a prompt call; otherwise the two-chance option would be in effect. The waving of arms or rackets designed to distract an opponent during play is strictly unethical. However, using subtle body feints is part of the sport and within the rules.

10. If a loose ball from an adjoining court comes to your court, wait until a temporary break in their play before returning the ball. Conversely, if one of your balls rolls into an adjoining court, wait until a break in their play before asking for it or retrieving it. Also, if you must cross another court in order to enter or exit from your court, do so only during breaks in play and always close the gates completely.

11. The server should always wait until the receiver is fully ready before serving. If a receiver feels the server has "quick served" him, the receiver should make no attempt to return the ball, and call a let.

12. Play should move along smoothly and continuously. In other words, any attempt at using stalling methods to disturb your opponent and the flow of play is considered unethical.

Along with the player's code, there are some unwritten rules of etiquette that should be included.

1. The server should always call out the score clearly. In this way, confusion and disagreements can be eliminated.

2. The server should always be supplied with balls. In order to keep the game going smoothly, both server and receiver should pick up balls between points.

3. Always bring your own practice balls. Don't be a moocher and expect others to supply the balls. If you have a regular practice partner, it is customary to alternate supplying the balls.

4. If you are on a public court without posted rules and

others are waiting, limit your play to 45 minutes. Don't be a court hog.

5. Control your temper. Not only is losing your temper detrimental to your own concentration, but it is rude to other players on your court and on adjoining ones.

Gamesmanship

Gamesmanship is the violation of the letter and spirit of the player's code and/or the unwritten rules of etiquette. Causing minor disturbances that don't exactly break any rules but are designed to distract one's opponent is a form of gamesmanship. For example, several years ago in a women's tournament in Massachusetts, I was playing a semifinal match. In the five-minute warm-up that was allotted, my opponent deliberately hit to the corners of the court for winners instead of keeping the ball in play by hitting to me. Therefore, in order to get a proper warm-up and keep a rally going, I would have had to run my tail off from corner to corner. I found myself starting to get very mad at this little bit of gamesmanship until I realized that that was exactly what she wanted me to do. It occurred to me that she wasn't getting any more of a warm-up than I, and I had already hit earlier in the day, so I wasn't so badly off. This thought calmed me down so that I could regain my concentration and composure. She went on to win a very close match, but it wasn't because she had succeeded in scrambling my brains. She was just better than I was that day. Thus, it's obvious that my opponent was not breaking any official rules; she was just trying to "get through to me," as the Australians on the circuit would say.

This example is unfortunately just one of many ways a player can indulge in gamesmanship, with or without officials present. Players can bounce the ball an inordinate number of times before they serve, they can stall in getting ready to return serve, tie their shoelaces at moments opportune for themselves, fake injuries, and many other things in the name of gamesmanship.

Gamesmanship Antidote

The antidote to gamesmanship is not in counterattacking with one's own games but in fighting back with greater honor, integrity, and concentration. First of all, it can be explained to a child that for a player to indulge in gamesmanship is a confession of a feeling of inferiority. That player must feel that he must resort to other means besides pure tennis to beat the child. With that perspective, it might then be easier for a child to rise above the situation and respond in a constructive way that would be beneficial to his own concentration. In the example when I realized my opponent's warm-up was no better than mine and that I was actually okay, I could then cool down and concentrate 100 percent, which is exactly what my opponent didn't want me to do. Thus, if a child can stop long enough to realize what his opponent's goal actually is (and it is always to win by ruining your concentration), then it is easier to take steps to thwart this goal. These steps are to stay within yourself, concentrate, and try your hardest to win. If opponents see that a child never "bites the bait," they will cease trying to use gamesmanship. As proof, just watch the king concentration-breaker of them all, Ilie Nastase, play against different opponents. With those people he knows he can't disturb, such as Stan Smith, Arthur Ashe, or Bjorn Borg, he keeps his antics down to a minimum. However, against more volatile opponents, as, for instance, John McEnroe or Sandy Mayer, he is merciless and at his worst.

Gamesmanship can actually have a backlash effect at times. In a match between Martina Navratilova and a top English player, Martina got very mad during the warm-up because her opponent would not hit the ball to her. Instead of Martina's anger interfering with her concentration, it spurred her on to concentrate and fight harder. She went on to demolish her opponent in straight sets. Thus, another way of coping with gamesmanship is to use that extra anger-induced energy to try harder, while still staying within yourself.

By "staying within yourself" we mean always keeping focused on your goals. In a tennis game your goals are generally to have fun, try your best, and win if you can. If you find yourself getting hot under the collar, and not from running, try taking some deep breaths and focus on your immediate goals. For instance, if your opponent is delaying the game and throwing a mini-temper tantrum at his end of the court, use that extra time to plan out the next few points, such as where exactly you'll return serve, which shot you'll play if the server comes to net, or which shot you'll hit if the server stays back. Don't look at your opponent while he's acting up. Bounce the ball on your racket, look at the ball while planning out your strategy, look anywhere but at your opponent. Thus, a child should be taught that he can become the victim of gamesmanship only if he allows it. A child controls his own concentration—no one else holds the reins—and the only way gamesmanship can win a match is if a child relinquishes control of his reins.

Cheating Antidote

In a way, the defense against overt cheating is simpler than gamesmanship because cheating is usually easier to detect, and there are rules against it. Generally, cheating takes the form of incorrect line calls or incorrect score reporting. In social tennis, if and when a child is confronted with a cheater we recommend that he put up with it that day and make a policy never to play with that person again. To get into arguments on the court would be futile, since a child is not going to change the other player's character or habits. Cheating is a result of deep-seated problems (often of overwhelming parental pressure), and a child is not going to effect any miraculous cure with one day of arguing.

If cheating occurs in a school, club, or tournament match, a child should stop the match, go to the main match desk, and ask for an umpire. Again, there is no sense in trying to argue or convince the other child to stop cheating because they will never admit it, may not be totally aware they are doing it, and may not be in enough control of themselves at that time to change it. However, a child should definitely not stay on the court and be victimized, either. Instruct children to take the matter where it belongs—to the hands of the officials.

Emotions

There is no doubt about the fact that competition can bring out strong emotions in participants of any age. Competition coupled with physical and mental exertion and fatigue is an extremely volatile combination. In tennis most players have learned to cope with these emotions so that they don't become a hindrance to their play. Other players have learned to channel these emotions in constructive ways so that they even help to energize them. Then there are some players who have failed to learn how to cope with their emotions and allow their outbursts to distract themselves and others around them. Players conducting themselves in this way are guilty of bad sportsmanship. Two important points to remember, though, are, first, that everyone has emotions, but it's how they are used that counts, and, second, that dealing with emotions is a learned behavior, not instinctual, and as such can be changed and modified.

Parents can help their children learn to cope with their emotions by describing specific guidelines for their behavior and setting clear limits. Barbara Jordan, a top touring pro from King of Prussia, Pennsylvania, who was coached by her father, is generally a model of proper court behavior. However, sometimes in practice she can allow her discipline to lapse and will throw mini-tirades on the court. Talking about her childhood and her father's reactions to her emotional displays she said:

> In a way, my dad was too good. Sometimes when I was acting up—screaming and shouting and throwing my racket—I wished that he would have told me to stop it. And I would have because I would only do what I thought I could get away with. I'd know he'd be mad at me because

he'd start feeding the balls harder at me and his face would get real set, but he'd never say anything.

Children need limits. They don't automatically know what is right or wrong, proper or improper, but must learn through trial and error.

It is pretty natural for youngsters to go through a temperamental stage, where they throw (and break) rackets, curse, and generally make fools of themselves. But this behavior is only a stage, if parents actively work to change it; otherwise a child will continue to do as much as he can get away with. I was never a very emotionally demonstrative person, but as a child I went through a brief phase of throwing temper tantrums on the court. The phase was brief because my mother soon put an end to it. She explained to me that if I ever behaved improperly on the court during a tournament match, she would stomp right on the court and yank me off. Knowing my mother's temper, I had no trouble believing her and soon learned to control my behavior.

Other players have had more painful lessons. Charlie Pasarell recalls an incident when he was fifteen years old and playing in an important tournament in Puerto Rico.

I always had a terrible temper as a little kid and I guess the biggest lesson I ever had from my father was one time when I was playing in a qualifying round robin for this real important tournament on the Caribbean circuit. I was playing a guy I used to have a lot of trouble with, a real steady player, and he got ahead about 4–1. I got very mad and slammed a couple balls across the net or something, and one nearly hit my opponent. My father was watching the match and ran on the court, grabbed me, took my rackets away from me and said, "That's it. You're defaulting this match." I said, "I can't default this match. I might miss qualifying in the tournament!" Then he said, "I don't care if I ever see you play tennis again if you're going to act that way." That's about all he said. I was in tears and had to default. He didn't make me pull out of the

192

tournament, which he was seriously thinking of doing, but he sure made it tough on me in that round robin. I just barely qualified for the event.

I sure remember that well, and I remember thinking, "If my father feels that ashamed of my behavior, maybe I shouldn't be doing that type of thing." It was hard because I cared so much about tennis and about doing well, and when I didn't perform well, I'd lose my temper.

Anyway, thank God I keep it somewhat under control. I mean, I lost my temper after that, but that incident always lingered in the back of my mind, so when I did lose my temper, I knew I was wrong and just tried to remember sooner for the next time.

Even Bjorn Borg, the ultimate stoic, has had to learn to curb his emotions. Borg told Peter Bodo for the July 1979 issue of *Tennis* Magazine,

> When I first started playing I was the worst. I was always throwing my racket. Sometimes even cheating, you know? Even cheating in practice with my friends. I wanted to win so badly. My parents were very disappointed, very embarrassed. They would shake their heads and say, "No way you will improve your game like that." I used to come home every day with the broken rackets. I was a madman.

Through his parents' guidance, and using Rod Laver as a model of self-control, Borg decided that unless he controlled his temper he would never become a great player.

Coping with Losing

Most, if not all, of the strong bad emotions in tennis revolve around losing. Players lose their tempers on court not so much because they are losing but because they start making the premature judgment that they have already lost. In calmer moments all players will agree that it's totally unreasonable to think they can always be ahead in a tennis match. The very essence and drama of the game is that the outcome is not known, and the opposing sides are constantly seesawing back and forth. Thus, winning and losing is part of the process of a tennis game, and they do not necessarily predict the final outcome. For example, in a recent tournament match I started out pretty shakily. I had been playing well in general, but on this day my game hadn't clicked into place. I knew that against this particular opponent I would have to hit the ball with some pace and not try to out-finesse her with softer shots. I also knew that, as poorly as I had started, if I just continued to hit out and go for my shots, perhaps making many errors and sacrificing points and games, my game might come together in time to win. With this mental attitude, losing for a time during the match was a necessary means to my desired end; I didn't make the mistake of thinking it *was* the end.

To understand this is a great help in controlling on-court emotions. A child can be taught to stay in the here and now and not jump to conclusions at any point in a match. A match is not lost because you're behind, nor won because you're ahead. Making those premature assumptions is a fatal mistake we have all made. The remedy is to do one thing at a time and take one point at a time. In this way a player's attention is focused on the here and now, leaving no time for any forecasting.

Another concept that would be helpful for a child to understand in dealing with on-court emotions is that the human organism functions at its best when in a relaxed yet alert state. To be psyched up—that is, eager, excited, and moderately nervous—is a good sign of readiness for action. However, when a player gets mad on court, he usually gets too excited and tense, which actually diminishes his physical and mental powers. Explain to children that keeping cool on the court is not just for appearances but will actually help them play better.

Another good reason a player shouldn't lose his temper on

court is that it helps out his opponent psychologically. If my opponent sees me getting mad because I'm losing, it only makes her think she's winning more than she thought she was. Then she gains confidence, hits out more, or fights harder to close it out, and I'm in bigger trouble than before. A child should be made to understand that most of the time it's better not to display any bad emotions to his opponent, to avoid giving that opponent a psychological boost.

Exceptions that should be mentioned are those emotionally charged people who have to let off steam in order to calm down. Billie Jean King, Jimmy Connors, and Pancho Gonzales are just such players. Although we're not advocating being temperamental, it is understandable that some people are more hot tempered than others and do need to act out a certain amount in order to release pent-up emotions. Often I've played doubles with Billie Jean and, if she's not playing as well as she wants to, I can see her anger mount during a match the more she tries to hold it in. Then, if there's a line call she doesn't agree with, she might explode briefly, feel much better, and go on to play better tennis. It should be noted that these players do try to control themselves within their limitations and, from my observation, play their best when they don't act up on court. But not every player can have the composure of a Borg or Austin, and to force a child into that mold may go against his emotional make-up. There is a range of behavior that should be held up as a standard. As Charlie Pasarell says, "I still lose my temper every once in a while, but I try not to and keep working on controlling it."

It Always Hurts

Once a player has lost, it's a different story. Emotions off the court are fine if they make you feel better. Some people are sulkers, others locker hitters, others merely quiet, and others appear fine, win or lose, but everyone hurts at least a little. That's okay, within limits. But after a cooling-off per-

195

iod, players should always analyze their loss. In this way a child can make the loss a learning experience and turn it into a long-term gain. This analysis need not be a gruesome point-by-point postmortem, but a child should have a good general understanding of why the match was lost. Parents can be helpful here by asking the right questions. Mrs. Austin recalls dealing with losses by her children.

I always try to be constructive after a loss. I'll ask if there was anything they could have done better, or if there's anything they could work on. Sometimes they'd say they didn't want to talk about it and I'd say, "I know it's painful, but if you just think it all through this time, you might be able to avoid this pain next time."

When a loss is treated this way, emotions are being dealt with constructively and the loss is not a long-term defeat, but merely part of an information-gathering experience to help the child in future games.

Emotions that Lead to Cheating

When emotions are not dealt with constructively, they can have a strong negative influence on a child that can lead to cheating. Also, how parents deal with their own emotions can greatly affect their children in positive or negative ways. Parents may get so caught up with the idea of winning that they make their children feel as though their parents' love is contingent on their winning. Alex Aitchison, vice-president and general manager of the Port Washington Junior Tennis Academy on Long Island, annually runs more than fifty junior events, small and large. In Barry Lorge's article, "Junior Tennis Isn't Child's Play" in *World Tennis* (June 1979), Aitchison complained,

Without a doubt, I have more trouble with the 12 and 14 age groups than any other, as far as cheating and temperament and court demeanor are concerned. It's a sorry state.
All that nonsense has got to stop, and I make a straight-

out appeal to parents of the bad actors to take control of them. Some of the parents don't realize it's them applying pressure by making the win so important that every point becomes a major crisis.

In the same article, Mrs. Austin explains:

We were careful not to put too much pressure on her [Tracy] . . . We never wanted her to feel she had to win to please us. Too many times it's the parents who want their child to be a champion, and that doesn't work. The child has to want it, to have the desire and the discipline to make the necessary sacrifices.

I've seen a few really bad cases of parental pressure to win, not only in tennis, but other sports. The kids know that if they lose, they're going to get it when they get home, so they'll do anything to win. And then there are some parents who know their children are cheating, and know that everybody else knows it, but never correct them because they'd rather have a winner than a good kid. I think those are the saddest cases of all.

The parents' desires, and the behaviors they choose to reinforce, greatly determine whether or not their child is going to cheat. If a parent is going to convey to the child the attitude that "I will love you only if you win," that parent will produce a cheater. On the other hand, if the parents' attitude is "I know it's important to you to win, but it's much more important to me that you play fairly," the child will not feel any parental pressure to win. In this way the child will feel accepted and loved, win or lose.

Another extremely important factor determining a child's fair play is what he learns from his parents, the role models. This includes not only how you conduct yourself in sports activities but how you conduct yourself in all your activities and relationships. Are you fair and just with your children in all ways? Do you have awful displays of temper? Do you conduct yourself with integrity in business? Parental characteristics, good and bad, will be absorbed by the children and determine to a great deal how moral a child will be.

A CHILD'S SPORTSMANSHIP is something that is taught by the parents, even if they know nothing of tennis. A child's coach can acquaint him with the written and unwritten rules, but whether or not a child follows them depends on the parents. The type of behavior parents encourage or discourage, the limits set for the child, the importance placed on fair play, and the types of behavior parents display as role models are the determining factors in a child's sportsmanship.

11.

Supportive and Pushy Parents

Because some of Nick's academy students live with him in his home, he is in an unusual position to observe their relationships with their parents.

I only wish you could hear some of the conversations on the telephone with the children talking to their parents. Some are terrific! "Mommy, I played today. I lost, but I played well. You just can't believe it, mother, but I really did play well. Oh, mother, I'm so glad you feel that way, thanks. I'll do better next time." The child is excited, eager to try again. They have no hesitation in calling their parents, no hesitation at all. The parents are happy the child is having fun, participating in a tournament, and doing fairly well.

But then I see those children who are afraid, actually afraid, to make a phone call. They get upset emotionally, lie about scores, or make up all sorts of excuses. Some are even upset about what their parents might do. And believe me, the penalties put on some of our athletes are amazing.

There are no clear and easy definitions that delineate pushy parents from supportive parents, because each parent-child relationship is totally unique. What may be supportive to one child is overbearing to another. Even within the same family this may be true. In this chapter we discuss in broad terms the range of behaviors between parents being unsupportive to being pushy, why parents get caught in traps that damage their relationships with their children, and how these traps may be avoided.

The Pushy Parent

The following item appeared in *Tennis* Magazine (February 1979):

Argentina's Claudia Casabianca, ranked No. 7 in the world among junior girls in 1978, was battling her opponent in a Buenos Aires tournament—and her father at the same time. After she lost a particularly painful point, her father stalked onto the court and slapped her. Claudia responded to this paternal incentive as you might expect: she lost the match.

Shocking, but true, and not all that uncommon. At the tournament level it seems as though each age-group category has a parent who actually resorts to physical punishment if his or her child loses. This is an extreme example of parents at their worst and of how intensely parents can get involved in their children's lives. However, less extreme parents can cause almost as much psychological pain in their children by exerting pressure in many subtle, covert, and even unconscious ways.

The pushy parent isn't hard to spot. He's the father forcing his son to take tennis lessons, the mother always sitting on the court watching her daughter practice, the father hovering over his daughter at tournaments, the mother boasting about how much her son wins, the father accusing his son's opponent of cheating, and on and on.

Parent Traps

The main traps these parents fall into is thinking that they know what is best for their children and that they are acting only in the best interests of their children. This line of reasoning is wrong on at least two counts. First of all, parents may *not* always know what is best for their children's de-

200

sires. Parents can suggest, explain, and recommend, but in matters that are not life or death, the child should make the ultimate decision, because he has to live it. Some of those decisions are going to be wrong, but that's okay, that's part of learning.

Second, parents may believe they are acting with their child's best interests in mind when actually their own unconscious needs and feelings of inadequacy may guide them to make the wrong choices for their child. A father may think it's extremely important for his daughter to learn a lifetime sport like tennis, but in reality the father may just be satisfying his own frustrated feelings to become a good athlete. Another consideration to take into account is that, by usurping a child's right to make decisions, a parent may be depriving him of the opportunity to learn how to make decisions. A child doesn't reach a certain age and then become fully capable of guiding his own life; he has to learn gradually while growing up.

Warning Signals from the Child

It is extremely difficult for parents to realize they're pushing because their intentions are good—they only mean well. Ask a pushy parent and a supportive parent if they love their child and they both say, "Very much." Yet one parent is causing his child great psychological pain and alienating the child, while the other is the child's partner in a happy life. Thus, to detect when one is being an overly pushy parent it is important to look for early warning signals in one's child and in one's own behavior.

In regard to seeing signals of excessive parental pressure in a young athlete, Nick recalls one particular student.

This one player is in her teens now and started playing when she was six years old. She was always very good, a tremendous athlete with great heart. She won many of the major junior championships in the United States, and always had a great desire to be number one in the United

States. However, along with her own strong desire always to win, her parents stressed that winning was the *only* thing in tennis.

In the early years of her career when she was winning consistently there were no family problems. However, as she got older and started experiencing a few more losses, she became quite frustrated and frightened of her parents' disapproval. She just didn't know how to cope with losses. As a result, every time a match got close, this girl would develop some physical symptoms, something would hurt her, or she just wouldn't feel well. Most of the time these could not be spotted by a doctor, so they were probably all in her mind. Eventually she even started calling lines wrong. Any ball that landed close to the line she would call in her favor. All of this was caused by her being made to believe that losing was totally unacceptable to her parents, so she would go to any lengths to avoid losing.

Often children who feel too much parental pressure will manufacture illnesses or injuries, in order to have an excuse if they lose. The parents of these children have somehow conveyed to them that winning is everything and is the only way to obtain parental approval and love. The child believes that losing is more acceptable if one is sick or injured.

When a parent stresses the "winning is everything" philosophy, the child can also develop other pressure symptoms besides physical ailments. The child can exhibit bad sportsmanship on the court in the form of cheating and outbursts of temper. Unconsciously in the child's mind he is losing not a tennis match but his parents' love. Thus, temper tantrums are a means of venting the frustration of losing that love, and cheating is a method of trying to avoid the tennis loss and subsequent loss of love. Other pressure signals include being afraid to lose or even talk about losses, lying about scores of matches, being afraid to compete, and eventually totally losing the motivation to play.

One last signal that may indicate that a child feels too much parental pressure is if he does not want his parents to watch him play. Feeling inadequate and unable to play up to his parents' expectations, a child would rather not play in front of them and risk failing them again.

One peripheral note: Another liability of pushing a child to win at all costs is that the techniques that might win for that child now are not the best ones to learn in the long run. A child may like playing tennis, but, due to parental pressure to win now, he neglects to learn the methods that may cause temporary losses but may be of great benefit later on. The child and parent may be appeased for the moment, only to run into a great deal of frustration and disappointment in later years.

These signals can also be caused by parents who force their child to play when he really doesn't want to. The frustration of being made to do something he doesn't want to do can be transformed into having the child's complaining of physical ailments, showing bad sportsmanship, and lacking any enthusiasm for the game. As Tony Trabert recalls,

> Yes, I saw quite a bit of the syndrome where the parent was really pushing the youngster, and as a result, when the kid got to be seventeen or eighteen, he would totally forget tennis. He wouldn't even play for fun. When you're a kid, you can't say anything because your parents are boss. But when you're an adult, you can look them in the eye and say, "I'm not doing it anymore, because I don't like it."

Warning Signals from Parents

Along with being alert for small signs indicating that a child feels pushed, parents can also look for signs in themselves. As Nick says,

> If parents don't push, they'll have a better time. If you get right down to it, it's the parents who are drinking too much, smoking two packs of cigarettes, arguing with their spouse, being impatient, leaving their businesses or duties too early to go to the courts to check on their child, and getting ulcers. If you have to push that hard to make

your son or daughter become a good tennis player, you're wasting your time. It's not worth it for you or your child. A sign that might indicate a parent's overinvolvement in his child's tennis is extreme nervousness over the child's matches. All parents are a bit nervous when their child is playing, but if they're getting headaches or showing other signs of stress, they may be going to an extreme. If a parent has to force a child to practice or go to lessons, if he finds himself getting mad or irritable if his child loses, or if he finds himself getting into arguments with his child or spouse over tennis, he should probably step back and see if he's pushing or getting too involved in the child's tennis.

Why Parents Push

There are several reasons why parents push their children, but the most fundamental one is low self-esteem in the parent. These parents see their children as extensions of themselves, instead of as separate individuals, and feel a boost to their own self-esteem when their children are successful in their endeavors. This type of parent thinks, "I wasn't as fortunate as my child, didn't have the same opportunities or helpful parents, but if I did, I would have been a good tennis player too. The fact that my child is winning is only confirmation of this." For this parent's child to win or play well is confirmation to that parent that he is doing a good job as a parent. In any case, it is the parent's need for validation, for a boost to his self-esteem that leads him to push his child to excel. Ironically, a parent's low self-esteem can be passed along to his child. The parent may give the child the idea that he could not succeed without the parent's help and efforts. The child then feels less than a full, self-sufficient person and feels dependent on the parent for successes in life.

Parents may also push their children to play tennis because they themselves would have liked to have been athletes. The scenario of the frustrated jock pushing his child into a sport in order vicariously to experience its thrills is almost a cliché, but is nonetheless true. The child is then only a tool to fulfill once again the parent's needs and bolster the parent's sagging self-esteem.

Another reason why a parent may push a child into tennis is to fill gaps in the parent's life. If the parent is feeling bored and empty and doesn't know what to do with his time, following and guiding a child's tennis career can add a lot of meaning to the parent's life. This is fine if the child wants to pursue tennis, and deadly if the child doesn't. Parents must be alert to their own needs and their children's needs, and not get the two confused. After all, a child's tennis career is only a temporary pursuit, and the parent will be left with the same problems once the child can go on his own.

Parents can also make the mistake of misjudging their child's abilities. It's very hard not to push a child you feel is going to be the next Bjorn Borg, but parents must realize how few such players there are in the world. They must also realize that Borg got where he is today because of his own desire, not that of his parents. It's wonderful that parents think their child to be the best, but not to the point where they put unrealistic expectations on the child. The child then feels like a failure rather than the recipient of a great deal of parental love.

How Parents Can Push

Just as there are many reasons why a parent will push a child, there are also many different ways of pushing, some more obvious than others. As mentioned, putting inordinate importance on winning can put a great deal of pressure on a child and give him a warped impression of what tennis or sports is all about. Showing unhappiness or even anger when a child loses quickly teaches him the lesson that a parent's love is contingent on winning tennis matches. Of course, verbal or physical punishment for losing is cruel and will earn a parent what he deserves—the child's alienation and dislike.

Another form of pushing is having unreasonable expectations of a child. If a parent feels his child is a superstar (when he is not) and expects him to show superstar results, the child will feel pushed to try to do more than he is capable of, which will result in a feeling of failure. A parent may think that he's doing his child's confidence a favor by raising his expectations, but if these expectations are too high, it might have a reverse effect.

Pushing can also be forcing a child to play, take lessons, and compete. If a child has to be forced to play, maybe he shouldn't play, an option often overlooked by parents. Interfering in a child's lessons and not letting the coach do his job is another form of pushing. Again, the parent is assuming that he knows what is best for his child, even more than the child or his coach may know. As far as a child's tennis career is concerned, this assumption is most often wrong.

How to Avoid Being a Pushy Parent

Those are just a few of the major ways a parent can push a child. In order to avoid falling into these behaviors, there are several things a parent can do.

1. Don't assume you know what your child's desires are. Talk and *listen* to your child and learn what his goals and desires are.
2. Let your child make decisions. There are many important decisions you must make for your child, such as whether or not he goes to school, gets a polio vaccination, enough sleep, and so on. These decisions are generally concerned with your child's survival and long-term well being. Matters of lesser importance outside of this sphere should be dealt with by your child—tennis being one of these matters. Because tennis is not a life-or-death matter, it is a good area in which your child can practice his decision-making abilities, make some mistakes, and learn how to be self-sufficient.
3. Deemphasize winning. Winning is wonderful, no doubt about it. However, there are many aspects to tennis

other than winning. Let your child know that you're proud of him regardless of the outcome, as long as he tried to the best of his ability. Your child should feel secure about your love without its being contingent on wins and losses. If your child feels secure and is happy playing tennis, winning will take care of itself. In fact, if a poll were taken of all the big winners in tennis, most would probably be able to repeat what Chris Evert says about her parents: "My parents would always tell me they loved me, win or lose. They just wanted me to try my best."

The Supportive Parent

There is a fine line between being supportive and being pushy. To not be pushy does not mean giving up all authority over a child or adopting a totally laissez-faire policy. After all, parents are the adults with greater knowledge and experience, and they can be extremely helpful in guiding a child and helping him make decisions. We do not feel that all parental pressure is bad, or even avoidable; we simply object to extreme amounts of pressure exerted in the wrong areas. To pressure a child to try hard in school and do all his homework is one thing; to push that child to feel that an A grade is the only acceptable mark is overstepping one's parental duties. In tennis, once a child has decided that he wants to play the game, parents can exert a certain amount of pressure to help teach the child the responsibilities of making such a commitment. We do not believe that a parent should pay for tennis lessons if the child will not practice. Parents can then insist that the child practice or reconsider his commitment. The child is then left with the choice of practicing or quitting altogether. Here lies a major difference between being pushy and being supportive: the pushy parent would not give his child any options—it would be practice or else. On the other hand, the supportive parent gives the child a choice, enabling the child to feel that he has control over his own life and that the parent's love is not contingent on that choice. As Nick comments,

> Life today is full of pressure, and it's darn good these kids are under pressure. But it must be legitimate pressure, pressure that will help mold them to be a complete person—not the kind of pressure that makes them feel defeated, or afraid to participate in sports.

How to Be Supportive Without Pushing

Probably the chief ingredients in being a supportive parent are unqualified love, involvement, and guidance. If your child feels 100 percent sure of your love, there is very little you can do wrong. Lauren Bacall, in her autobiography *By Myself,* talks of the love she felt from her mother,

> She always made me feel that I could do anything once I made up my mind. She started me in dancing school when I was three. Yet she was not pushy—anything but a stage mother . . . [when I was twelve] she didn't see that I was tall for my age, underdeveloped for my age, and had feet too big for the rest of me. Through her belief in me and her abounding love for me, she convinced me that I could conquer the world—any part of it or all of it. Whatever I wanted.

A child should be able to feel he can go out and succeed or fail at his chosen endeavors without the risk of losing a parent's love or causing a parent unhappiness. As Martina Navratilova remembers,

> My parents never made me feel that my winning or losing was responsible for their happiness. In fact, sometimes when I won, but misbehaved on the court, my father would spank me. And then sometimes I'd lose, but try really hard and my father would tell me I did well and that he was proud of me.

Loving a child for himself for his qualities as a human being, not for his sports accomplishments, is the most important part of being a supportive parent.

Another facet of being supportive is taking an interest in your child's activities, being involved to a degree. Billie Jean King talks about her parents' involvement in her tennis.

My parents were always supportive, but never interfering. In fact, they gave more time to Randy [Randy Moffitt, her brother, is a relief pitcher for the San Francisco Giants] because they were more familiar with baseball. But they had to spend a lot of time on me, getting me to my practices and tournaments. They really sacrificed a lot of their own time to help me out.

Even a young player like Ben Testerman, the number two ranked junior in the United States, already understands the help he receives from his parents.

My parents are real supportive. If I wanted to quit tomorrow, they wouldn't encourage it, but they would respect my decision. My parents helped me more than anyone—keeping me going, helping out with unbelievable amounts of money. My mom traveled with me, showing me right from wrong.

Conversely, when parents don't get involved, their child's enthusiasm for a sport may die. Tracy Austin's mother feels that tournaments are a great incentive for children to get out and practice. Therefore, she feels it's a parent's duty to make sure his child gets to play as many tournaments as he wants to. Mrs. Austin recalls: "I knew a mother who wouldn't drive her child to tournaments. So her daughter eventually lost interest in tennis—she had no motivation to practice, no goals."

Involvement and guidance are often closely interrelated. Parents generally have a better perspective of the big picture and can help their child stay on the track the child has chosen. As Tracy Austin says,

209

My parents did such a good job. They knew exactly how much to push and how much not to push. I don't really like to say push because you might interpret it the wrong way. They just pushed me a little bit in the beginning. Sometimes I'd just be lazy and want to go play in the sandbox, but my parents would have me hit balls. Or I wanted to stay out late during a tournament and my parents wouldn't let me. I really started to enjoy tennis and now I'm really glad they gave me a push in the beginning.

Some mothers drive me bananas because I see them pushing their kids so hard. They hit their kids balls, keep them out on the court for hours and scream and yell at them. The kids are crying and you know by now they hate tennis. As soon as these kids can quit tennis, you know they're going to quit.

Mrs. Austin adds this about the guidance she gave her children:

I'd push them to get their practice partners lined up for the whole week by Sunday. If they didn't, then Wednesday would come along and they wouldn't have anyone to practice with. So I would nag them about that. I also thought it was important to enter as many tournaments as possible. We'd go off every weekend to a tournament and let them take their lumps. Kids motivate themselves for tournaments, so we didn't have to push at all. If they lost to a kid one week, they wouldn't want to lose again, and they'd go out and practice in order to beat that kid next time.

Charlie Pasarell and his parents had philosophies similar to Tracy's and her parents'.

The point is that parents have to be there, they just can't let you do whatever you want. That's not going to work. The parent has to take an interest in what the child is doing, but it's more like encouragement, not pushing.

If I said to my parents I was tired and didn't want to practice anymore, they'd say, "Fine." At the same time, if I said I didn't want to play today, and then the next day, by the fourth day they would say, "Wait a second. If you want to go play tournaments this summer, you'd better start getting back to the tennis court. It's your choice." I knew I wanted to go to the U.S. and play tournaments, so I knew I better go out and practice.

They gave me a certain amount of direction, you know? I never felt in my life that my parents ever pushed me into anything. They always pointed things out to me and steered me in the right way.

The degree of urging or pushing is extremely important, but so also is the manner. Tony Trabert explains how his father was able to push him without being offensive.

If the youngster wants to be a good player, then the parent should encourage and push a little bit to get them to the courts. I went through one stage when I was about fourteen or fifteen when to get to the club I would have to take a bus and a streetcar, and walk about a mile. Sometimes on a summer day my pals were playing baseball, so I'd go out with them instead of to the club. So my dad figured out a way he could take me to the club on his way to work and pick me up after work. I wasn't playing from eight in the morning to eight at night, but I was playing plenty because I was there. I could take a lesson if someone cancelled and I used to have lunch with the pro. So my dad figured out a way to get me to the courts without it being unattractive to me.

I always felt that if I wanted to quit, my father would have let me. The only requirement dad had was that I try and make a commitment, that if I wanted to play tennis, I should do it right. He wanted me to understand that If I wanted to be a good player, I would have to practice hard, train hard, and not go halfway.

What is important to note is that all the above-mentioned players loved tennis and had a desire to excel in it. These feelings were not instilled in them by their parents. So for these players' parents to push them a bit to practice is totally different from a situation where parents are pushing their children to play when they have very little interest in tennis. The key is that parents should work within their child's goals and ambitions, not their own. Parents must find out what their child's goals are and then help the child devise and carry out a plan to accomplish these goals. However, within this framework it is the parents' role and obligation to set limits and duties for the child. Children can be short-sighted and need parental guidance to stay on the track toward their longer-term goals. For example, Charlie Pasarell's goal was to be a very good tennis player; his desire was to play tournaments. His parents, understanding Charlie's goals, made sure he carried out the necessary actions—that is, practicing and training—that would help him accomplish his goals. Jimmy Connors wanted to be the best tennis player in the world, and his mother has helped him try to attain his goal. However, if Mrs. Connors interacted with another child who had lesser or different desires, she might have been too overbearing or pushy. But because she worked with Jimmy within his own framework, he did not perceive her as being pushy, just supportive and helpful.

PARENTAL INVOLVEMENT in a child's tennis is desirable and should be encouraged. Loving a child unconditionally, showing interest in his activities, and guiding him in ways that help him attain his goals are all part of being a supportive parent. On the other hand, forcing a child to work toward goals that a parent sets is risking making the child's life unhappy and alienating his affections. Parents can slip into this trap out of their own feelings of inadequacy, misapprehension of their child's abilities, or need to make their own lives more interesting or meaningful. Being a supportive parent is an ongoing process that requires parents to take constant inventory of their actions and motives regarding their children. They should always try to be alert to any early warning signals from themselves or their children that can tip them off to any discord in their relationship with their children. Judging from the severe consequences of being a pushy parent (turning a child off tennis entirely, damaging the relationship with a child), to err in the direction of not being involved enough seems like the safer path to take.

12.

Tennis and a Child's Schooling

Parents often ask of their child's involvement in tennis "Will tennis interfere with my child's academic career?" Parents are afraid that the time spent on the court will not only take their child away from the books but sap their child of energy needed for more scholarly pursuits. In regard to this issue we are in agreement with John F. Kennedy, who said, "Intelligence and skill can only function at the peak of their capacity when the body is healthy and strong." We feel that in the majority of cases tennis will only be an aid to a child in school, increasing his energy and strength, and helping him to learn good study habits.

A less frequent concern of some parents is the question of whether or not school interferes with their child's tennis. With a very few college-age youths who are fortunate enough to have a promising tournament career, the tough choice exists either to enter college and subordinate or delay a tennis career, or to forego college and pursue only tennis. We maintain that just as tennis need not interfere with a child's school, school need not interfere with a child's tennis. The two endeavors are far from mutually exclusive, and, in fact, can be complementary. In this chapter we explore this relationship.

A Case Study

The best example I can think of to illustrate a harmonious blend of tennis and school in a child's life is myself. Since I was eight, both tennis and school have been quite important in my life. Although in obtaining a Ph.D. my academic career has been longer than most pros', my experiences have not been that unique. Many of the top players in the United States, such as Julie Heldman, Barbara Jordan, Arthur Ashe, Stan Smith, and Charlie Pasarell have been able to combine a successful tennis career with a college education. A child may not wish to become an academician or professional tennis player, but many of the experiences he will have with school and tennis will be similar to many of my past experiences.

I was nine when I started competing in local tournaments. By the time I was fifteen I had attained a high ranking in southern California and was offered a full academic and tennis scholarship to Westlake School, a private girls' school in Los Angeles with an excellent academic record and a good tennis team. Although I was a good student, the main reason Westlake wanted me was to help build up their tennis team. As part of their admissions procedure I had to be interviewed by the vice-principal. It was during this interview, when I had to answer questions on how I managed to find time for both school and tennis, that I realized how much tennis helped me academically.

Because school and tennis took up so much of my time, I learned from an early age to be well organized. If I had a paper due in two weeks, I couldn't postpone getting started on it, because in one week I might have a tournament on the weekend taking up most of my time. I just didn't have the leeway to procrastinate and then cram for an exam or paper, because I had very little extra time. In this way I learned that if I planned ahead and paced my schoolwork I could get everything done without too much hassle. Conversely, if I had a tournament coming up, I knew I should make time to practice every day in preparation. So, in order to avoid having a big lump of homework on any one day that would prevent me from practicing, I learned to do my homework as it was assigned, use the time given me in study halls to get down to work, and catch bits and pieces of time during the day to get some work done. I don't mean to give the impression that I was all business and no play; far from it. I just had less time than other kids to waste and goof off, and, maybe, get into trouble.

Another major contribution tennis made to my academic life was in the area of study habits. First of all, in tennis I learned that I couldn't expect miracles—if I didn't practice, I couldn't expect to improve and win matches. It was easy to use the same line of reasoning with my schoolwork. I knew I had to practice (do my homework) in order to make good grades. Getting good grades was not a result of being a "brain" but of simply putting in the "practice" time and doing my homework. Another thing I learned through tennis was that my weaknesses would get better only if I worked on them. I couldn't avoid hitting backhands and expect my backhand to improve. In the same way, I knew that the school subjects I didn't like or did poorly in could not be ignored. I realized that those were the subjects I had to spend extra time on in order to improve and gain some confidence in them, which also made me like them more.

What I didn't know at the time I went to Westlake, but learned when I was at Stanford, was how much playing tennis added to my overall energy level. For one quarter at Stanford I decided to forego tennis and concentrate only on my studies. Instead of having more energy to study, I found I had less, got tired and lost my concentration more quickly. Without being aware of it, tennis had increaed my stamina not only for tennis but for other things, including studying. Instead of tennis sapping my limited energy, it actually added to my ability to study for longer periods of time.

Other benefits I experienced in high school as a result of my tennis were being able to travel to school tournaments and develop close friendships with other members of my team. Traveling with my team and the school's tennis coach gave me an opportunity to be somewhat on my own and independent of my parents for short periods of time, while still being well supervised. These opportunities are terrific for kids, because they provide a gradual way for children to get used to coping without their parents before they have to face the more extreme condition of going away to camp for a whole month or going off to boarding school or college. Also, having teammates who shared the same problems of combining a tennis hobby with a school career was an incentive to me, showed me I wasn't alone in my problems, and showed me that it all could be done. Needless to say, some of my teammates became some of my best friends.

Another academic benefit that befell me as a result of being involved in tennis was that being an active tennis player made it easier to get into the college of my choice. In 1965, Stanford wanted not only good students but people who were well rounded and interested in other activities. If they had a choice between two A students and one was an accomplished violinist, they would choose the violinist. Not all schools have such an admissions philosophy, but being a well-rounded student could certainly never hurt. Today, being a good tennis player not only looks good on a high school record but can lead to a college athletic scholarship, whether you're male or female. In 1965, there were very few athletic scholarships for women, and even fewer to any college or university that was highly ranked academically. Times have changed for the better and today athletic scholarships exist for both men and women to many of the top universities in the country.

Finally, I discovered that to earn money to help pay for my college education I could use my tennis background to get jobs teaching at tennis camps during the summer. In fact, years later, when I had turned pro and was attending graduate school, giving private tennis lessons was my main source of income and paid for my education.

In my life, which I think is a fairly typical example, tennis was far from being an interference with my schoolwork. To a great extent it is because of tennis that I learned to become organized, developed good study habits, and maintained good physical stamina to carry out all my activities. Besides these benefits, tennis gave me the opportunity to travel, make close friendships with teammates, get into the college of my choice, and earn money to help pay for my education.

The Poor Student, Good Player

You might be thinking, "That's all well and good if your child is a good student, but my child is just average and probably won't have the same experiences." What are the possible consequences of an average or poor student getting involved in tennis? Tennis cannot hurt a child's schoolwork and can actually be of help in the areas mentioned. Parents can be of help in showing their children the similar ways in which tennis and school can be approached. A child may well know that he has to hit a bucket of serves every day to improve that stroke, but he may not have made the connection yet that he has to plug away at English grammar every day to gain a good understanding of the subject.

If a child is really in love with tennis to the extent that he takes time away from studies to devote to tennis, a parent may have to intervene and set some ground rules. A helpful approach is to set up contingencies. For example, for every hour a child plays tennis, he must spend an equal number of hours doing homework. Or a child may go away to a tournament for the weekend if he does a certain amount of extra homework. These "deals" mean a certain amount of extra work for the parent in the form of overseeing the child fulfill his end of the deal, but the end result is that the parent knows his child is not neglecting his homework in favor of tennis.

The biggest benefit tennis has for the average or poor student is in helping him get into college and perhaps receive a tennis scholarship. Many colleges will accept students with grades that fall below their usual standards, if that student will be a significant addition to the college's tennis team. A child may be a late academic bloomer, and, once in college, may be stimulated scholastically and become a better student.

The Excellent Student, Excellent Player

The child who excels in both tennis and school seems to have the best of all possible worlds—and he does, up to a point.

The only problem for this child is the number of options available to him. Today the choices are much tougher than they were when I was of high school age. When I was sixteen there was no doubt in my mind that I was going to go to college. School was always my main occupation and tennis always my hobby. Professional tennis for women didn't exist then, and even among the men's professional ranks there were precious few spots available. Tennis did not yet have tournaments open to both amateurs and professionals with substantial prize money, so it was not very feasible for a young player to think he could make a good living playing tennis. All that has changed drastically, to the extent that a professional tennis career is now extremely alluring to many young players. Since a talented young player reads that sixteen-year-old Tracy Austin won $356,343 in prize money in her first year as a pro, it's very hard to convince that youngster that he should continue his education. For an extremely rare few youngsters, they probably shouldn't. The choices are tough.

One important factor a child should consider before shutting his mind to further schooling is that youngsters like Austin, Pam Shriver, and Andrea Jaeger have already proven themselves against the very best. They know they can survive and do well in professional tennis because they've been there. If these youngsters choose not to go to college, they know they can make it in tennis. Unless a child has actual proof that he can realistically compete against the best, then staying in school is the better choice.

Another consideration is that the continuation of a high school or college education does not eliminate the possibility of carrying on a tennis career simultaneously. There are numerous examples of youngsters—Tracy Austin, Pam Shriver, Jimmy Arias, Ben Testerman, Scott Davis, and Kathleen Horvath—all top juniors nationally, who are good students and also maintain a heavy tournament schedule. There are many other top players—Sandy Mayer, Barbara Jordan, and Julie Heldman—who managed to graduate from a tough university like Stanford and still play the highest caliber international tennis. In fact, if the college or university has a strong tennis program (and many schools now do), the years spent playing college tennis can help mature a child's game and offer a transition stage between junior and professional tennis. If a youngster is in doubt about whether to pursue a tennis or academic career, choosing to go to college may be a way of having your cake and eating it too. If the child chooses a college that suits him academically and athletically, he can continue to work toward his tennis goals while getting a taste of academia. After a year or so, a teen-ager may want to reconsider his choice, but at least he has more information to go on.

Two young adults who went through just such a process were Kathy and Barbara Jordan. Today both play full-time professional tennis, Kathy at twenty-one ranked number ten in the world, and Barbara at twenty-three ranked number fifty-eight. Both women attended Stanford University, Barbara graduated, and Kathy completed a little over two years. Kathy entered Stanford knowing she wanted to play college tennis, but she didn't know whether she was good enough to play professionally. Playing against her teammates, who were some of the best collegiate players in the country, and playing many intercollegiate tournaments gave Kathy the idea that she could hold her own, at least at that level. Winning both the singles and doubles (with Barbara) events at the prestigious A.I.A.W. (Association for Intercollegiate Athletics for Women) Championships, and winning a pro-circuit satellite tournament as an amateur, planted the idea in Kathy's head of being a professional player. Kathy continued to do well in pro tournaments and finally decided to leave school, turn pro, and play full-time. The decision was a tough one, because Kathy really enjoyed Stanford and her friends there, and still thinks she may go back to finish one day.

Barbara's experience at Stanford was slightly different, because she did not do well in the pro tournaments until later in her college years. By then she had decided that she might as well finish her schooling and then play full-time.

220

The main disadvantage for her while at Stanford was that, between playing on the school team and taking her required courses, she didn't have time to take other subjects she was interested in. But today Barbara is glad she finished Stanford, because now she has her degree and is still able to play professional tennis. Thus, it is apparent from the experiences of these two women that for the excellent student player a harmonious blend of school and tennis can be found without sacrificing either one.

How to Choose a College for Tennis

Choosing a college is a very important matter in a youngster's life. Many factors, such as academic quality, athletic quality, financial costs, locale, and social life have to be carefully analyzed. Parents can help their child by pointing out all the factors to be considered and helping him focus on all possible short- and long-term goals. If selecting a college for its tennis program is important to a child, there is an organized way of going about it. Here are some important points to take into consideration when choosing a college.

1. *Coaching* Is the coach qualified and experienced? Is the coach a good instructor and can he motivate the players? Does he have the necessary knowledge to get players on national teams (Junior Davis Cup, Junior Federation Cup) and into important tournaments? What do present and past team members say about him or her?
2. *Facilities* Are there enough tennis courts, and are they in good condition? Do team members get to use the courts enough? Are there indoor facilities available on campus or in the community for periods of inclement weather? Is there more than one type of court surface available? Are there facilities for supplemental training (track, weight lifting)?

3. *Team members* Do they offer you good competition? Are they too good, so that your chances of making the team are slim? Are they available for practice?
4. *Match schedule* Which are the match seasons? Do you compete against good schools? Do you travel, or compete locally or regionally? Does the schedule allow you time to play individual tournaments to build up your personal record?
5. *Practice schedule* Are there regular practices throughout the year? Are practices well organized? Are they competitive? Are they tough enough or too tough? Are they well supervised?
6. *Scholarships* Are scholarships available? Do they provide for tuition, room, and board? Are they hard to get?
7. *Tournaments* Is the college in an area where there are local tournaments? Would it be feasible for you to enter these tournaments?
8. *Weather* In general, is the weather to your liking? Is it conducive to playing tennis?
9. *Additional practice and professional help* Are there players in the community with whom you can practice? If you need extra coaching help, is there a good coach in the vicinity?

A child should have definite opinions on all these major points and continue searching for a school that can meet all of his requirements. A child should be picky about this decision and be persistent in looking for a school that's just right for him.

College Scholarships

College tennis scholarships have existed for decades for men, but have only recently been available to women. The fortunate timing of the tennis boom with Title IX legislation, which prohibits sex discrimination in all educational institutions receiving federal aid, is primarily responsible for the rapid growth of women's college tennis and, in turn, of tennis scholarships. Today, nationwide, there are about 1,100 full or partial tennis scholarships for women players and nearly 1,400 full or partial scholarships for men. Eve Kraft, director of the U.S.T.A.'s Education and Research Center, says,

It's important to realize that these scholarships for women are being offered by many different kinds of schools, from junior and community colleges to small liberal arts colleges, to state and private universities throughout the country. They're not just Stanford, USC, or Trinity, where the tennis team rosters read like a list of "women pros of tomorrow." There are as many levels of collegiate competition as there are levels of the game, so the varsity high school player, even without a national or high sectional ranking, stands a good chance of making a college team and having at least part of her expenses paid. She just has to be realistic in her choice of schools and find the right niche where she won't have to warm the bench, but also won't be without tough competition for her particular game.

For a complete list of available college tennis scholarships and how to go about applying for them, write for the U.S.T.A. College Tennis Guide, U.S.T.A. Publications, 729 Alexander Road, Princeton, New Jersey 08540.

How to Get a Tennis Scholarship

There are four principle steps in obtaining a tennis scholarship: choosing a college, contacting the coach, visiting the school, and having an interview.

1. *Choosing a college* We have just covered the major steps in selecting a college, but we urge you to be honest with yourself about both your academic and tennis abilities. Unreasonable self-perceptions will only make you suffer in the long run. Also, make a list of several colleges that you would like to attend.

2. *Contacting the coach*   Write directly to the tennis coaches. You should include the following information: personal goals, a resumé, photo, team record in high school, state, regional, and/or national ranking, significant wins, grade-point average, test scores, and a letter of recommendation from a person who would be meaningful to a coach, such as a tennis pro or another coach. If appropriate, be sure to include your specific needs for financial help.

3. *Visiting the school*   Make sure you watch the team practice and if possible, play a match. Talk to the team members and get their opinions of the tennis program. What is the general attitude of the team—casual, competitive, lazy, hardworking? Do you feel you could blend in?

4. *The interview*   Make sure *you* talk to the coach, not your parents. Be honest; you're not trying to please the coach, you're trying to find a coach and school that are compatible with you and your goals. Have specific questions prepared.

After completing these steps, give yourself time to think. Generally, visiting a college campus can be a real "turn-on," and you may overlook things that in a less excited mood you might object to. If you have been offered scholarships, once you have chosen the school let the other colleges know of your decision immediately, so they can offer their scholarship to another student. Also, let the school of your choice know immediately, so they can use your name for publicity and further recruiting. If you are waiting to hear about receiving a scholarship, ask the school for a reasonable deadline, and keep in contact with the coach so he knows how interested you are. Lastly, before accepting a scholarship, be certain you are willing to fulfill the school's and coach's expectations. They want a serious tennis player who will be a significant addition to their tennis team. Are you willing to meet that obligation?

BEING INVOLVED in tennis should not be harmful to a child's schooling. In fact, through tennis a child can learn many valuable lessons in organization and study habits, as well as improve his overall stamina, which can help his concentration span. Whether a child is a poor, average, or superior student, there is a place in his life for both school and tennis. Tennis can be a great asset to any caliber student, helping the youngster get into the college of his choice and perhaps helping in obtaining a scholarship. There are many different colleges offering a variety of academic and tennis programs. With careful analysis and preparation, a child can find just the right school for himself.

13.

Should a Child Compete?

My brother Gary and I started competing in tournaments at the same time, a year after we both started playing. I was nine and he was thirteen. Our age difference was just large enough to make the type of competition we each had to confront vastly different. Gary had to play some boys who already had three, four, and five years of tournaments under their belts, but I was playing against girls who had been playing for approximately the same length of time. Thus, after a few months, while I started winning some matches, my brother continued losing, and losing, and losing. Another difference between us was how we adapted to competition. I thrived on it, loved to win, was heartbroken when I lost, but always looked forward to playing. In contrast, competition was agonizing for Gary. He worried about upcoming tournaments, got extremely jittery the day of matches, and, more than once, lost his breakfast before stepping on the court.

Looking back, I realize that the differences in our reactions to competition had less to do with any basic personality or talent differences than with the differences in our early experiences with competition. While I at least met with some early successes, Gary faced one loss after another. Had Gary been able to experience winning more often at the beginning, his whole attitude and outlook regarding competition might have been different. If my parents had been a little more knowledgeable about tennis, they might have entered Gary in some extremely easy tournaments, where he could have won some matches. With some wins, he could have faced tougher competition with more confidence. In this way he might have grown to like the whole process of competition better.

There are personality differences among children in their reactions to competition, but the most important factor determining their outlook is their early experience with competition. Competition is an unavoidable fact of life. Some people may not like it, but it's impossible not to deal with it. A child competes every day, on the playground, in the classroom, in the home. Thus, rather than pretend it doesn't exist, parents can help a child learn to deal with competition in a manner best suited to him. Competition in itself is neither good nor bad, but how it is dealt with is. Tennis offers a child an opportunity to learn how to cope with competition in a way that will be beneficial to him in later life in many different areas. In this chapter we discuss the pros and cons of competition, why some children fear it, and the overall gains and losses for a parent.

Benefits of Competition

There's no doubt about it—competition promotes excellence. IBM produces the best computers in the world because they're trying to stay ahead of more than 150 other computer companies nipping at their heels. The more intense the competition, the better the products. Running records are broken when the race is close and the competition strong, not when one runner leads by a mile. Competition can bring out the best possible tennis game that is within a child. Few reasons motivate a child more to practice and improve than the prospects of winning a meaningful match. Even now the difference in my game when I'm playing tournaments and when I'm not is huge, not because I spend any more time on the court but because competition forces me to concentrate harder and be that much sharper.

Just as competition motivates players to practice, it teaches them to set and strive for realistic goals. "Sally might have beaten me this tournament, but I'm going to get her next one." "I may only be ranked number 30 this year, but I'm going to work on my volley and be number 20 next year." Competition gives a child tangible yardsticks to measure his progress. If the goals are unrealistic, it's obvious. If I aimed to be number 1 this year, but was only number 25, I know I would have to alter my thinking. Competition thus provides a structure in which a child can learn to formulate goals and receive feedback on the realism of those goals.

Competition teaches decision making under pressure, and the pressure is the legitimate, honest, simple pressure of pure rivalry, not the damaging kind exerted by parents. A child has learned certain techniques and strategies in the relaxed atmosphere of practice sessions. Now he can learn through trial and error how to choose the right tactics, how to think when it really counts.

In competition a child has an opportunity to be moral under pressure. Anyone can be magnanimous in giving his opponent the benefit of the doubt in a practice match, but what do people do on match point in a tournament? A child will not know right from wrong automatically, but in situations that parents can observe, he will be tested, make mistakes (which we hope will be corrected by parents), and, as a result, become a better person. The lessons a child learns on the tennis court will not remain within the bounds of that rectangle but will permeate his entire life and influence his morality at school, at home, and at play, now and in the future.

Competition provides an arena for a child to face defeat and failure and rebound from it. To a young child, losing a tennis match can be devastating. I can still vividly remember sobbing in my mother's arms after losing my very first tournament match. I thought my brief tennis career had come to a tragic end. However, it didn't take me long to learn that there was always another tournament somewhere. Losing never became easy, but I learned to think of it as a temporary setback rather than an end to all my aspirations. I also found out that my opponents could make me aware of my weaknesses much more strikingly than could my coach. Using that information helped me in my practice sessions when preparing for the next tournament. In this way I was using a process that Nick calls "turning a loss into a win."

Finally, competition puts a child among good company. Serious athletes are generally too busy to get into trouble and have too much respect for their bodies to abuse them. As seventeen-year-old Ben Testerman says,

> Most of my friends are athletes because I think they're good influences. They're clean livers. I like to go to school parties, but I don't like to stay out very late. I don't drink or smoke and I don't like to be around kids that drink and smoke and party all night. I like beer, but I don't drink it because I'm an athlete, and I like to be religious about that.

Disadvantages of Competition

Ninety-nine percent of the disadvantages of competition come from parents mishandling their children. Parents can make their child's competitive experiences 100 percent positive or 100 percent negative. Parents should ask themselves: "Do you overemphasize the importance of winning?" "Do you gloat and brag about wins?" "Do you respond to a loss with anger, disgust, bitter disappointment?" "Do you see a loss as being a tragedy?" Far stronger than any words or lectures, a parent's behavior conveys his philosophy of winning and losing to his child. And, unfortunately, your child is the victim of your poor philosophy. The greatest danger in competition for a child is if the parent has a bad attitude and makes the child fear competition, fear the parents' reaction to losses, and makes the child feel like a failure. In assessing whether or not competition is going to be damaging or helpful to a child, parents must honestly analyze their own attitudes. If they are sure that in thought, word, and action they can make their child feel loved, despite any score or ranking, then the child can only benefit from competition.

There are other disadvantages of competition, but they are possible only if parents are unaware of their existence and fail to deal with them properly. A prepared and forewarned parent can turn these possible disadvantages into advantages and learning experiences. One of these possible pitfalls is for your child to lose his perspective regarding tournaments. For an eleven year old who has spent an hour every day practicing for a tournament and who loses in the first round, his misery knows no bounds. A child can get so involved with competing that he may attach his self-esteem to wins and losses. If the child wins a match, he may be insufferable, thinking the world has never seen such a star. Conversely, if this child loses he feels like a failure, a worthless person. Thus, parents have to be ready to make clear to their children that tennis is just a part of their total life, and how they're judged as human beings has nothing to do with their tournament results. When I lost a match, my parents would say, "Sorry, honey, there's always next time. We still love you a lot." When I won they would say, "That's great, honey, congratulations! But remember, there's always someone out there a little bit better." My parents made it very clear to me that whether or not I was a tennis star, what counted in their books was whether or not I was a kind and decent human being.

Another disadvantage of competition is that it can be very stimulating to a child who perhaps doesn't have the ability to match his ambitions. A child can be so turned on by tournaments that he will want to become number 1 in the world, when the realistic chances of that happening are infinitesimal. Two things are possible here. First of all, through pure persistence and determination this child could win many matches. Ilie Nastase (number 52 in the world) has all the talent in the world and squanders it with a lack of mental discipline. Harold Solomon (number 8 in the world) and Eddie Dibbs (number 10 in the world) have half Nastase's ability but double the determination, and win far more matches because of it. Second, this child might be forced to alter his expectations by the hard facts of tournament results. If he aspires to be number 1, but can't qualify for the state tournament, the reality of his situation is bound to hit home. There are, however, those situations where a coach or parent has to set the child down and be very honest and frank. As Nick notes,

It's extremely tough, but in the long run it's much better for the kids to know my absolute honest opinion of their chances. These kids don't have to abandon tennis altogether, just alter their sights somewhat. Being a pro player may be out of the question, but making a high school team or becoming a teaching pro may be reasonable alternatives.

There is certainly no reason to discourage an untalented kid from playing. Mrs. Austin remarks,

I've seen a lot of tennis parents in southern California who know their children are never going to be world champions. They see they're just not that talented, but they encourage them because it keeps the kids active and interested in something that will be healthy and enjoyable their whole lives.

Or, as Billie Jean King says, "Doing the best you can do with the equipment you have is winning."

Making certain sacrifices is another possible disadvantage of competition, especially for the very serious player. Ben Testerman explains.

You have to make choices. I really wanted to go to Ft. Lauderdale with my friends over Easter rather than go to Caracas for a tournament, but I figured playing on the beach in Florida wouldn't help me win Wimbledon. In a way you sacrifice a lot, but in a way you don't, 'cause you hope it'll pay off in the future.

Tony Trabert has a slightly different point of view.

I never felt I had to make sacrifices, because I was doing what I like to do. So when I would train, run up and down the steps in the football stadium, run miles, jump rope, exercise, and practice for hours, I was doing it because I wanted to. Nobody was forcing me to do it. As an example, in high school I didn't go steady with any girl because when a weekend tournament came up, I wanted to go play tennis—I didn't want to worry about the dance Saturday night. So I played the field and had no particular ties. I guess my dancing suffered. They call me suction cup now. I spent all my time running on tennis courts, so a two-step is all I can do.

What some people might have seen as sacrifices Ben and Tony did not. If a child is doing what he really wants to do and is not being forced or pressured into it by anyone else, he will not feel deprived in any way.

For those few children who are tennis prodigies there is one other possible disadvantage of competition. Because of the enormous amounts of money and fame for tennis players, the temptation is great to develop a gifted youngster quickly. The obvious pitfall of too much parental pressure then becomes possible. Some kids weather the tough competition well. These are the ones we read about. Other children may need a more relaxed atmosphere in which to develop their games. Chris Evert warns,

> The experience of playing the top pros is great, as long as the results are good and a player's development doesn't suffer. But there's really no need to rush onto the tour. I used the years between fourteen and seventeen to develop my game, working four to five hours a day.

This advice is particularly poignant today after Chris's announcement at age twenty-five to quit the tour indefinitely because she felt tired and burned out. Imagine how she might have felt had she started playing it and doing well at fourteen, as Tracy Austin did!

Another pitfall for the prodigy is being pampered too much by parents, officials, organizers, and equipment representatives. As Arthur Ashe explained to Barry Lorge (*World Tennis*, June 1979),

> I see a trend toward the pampering of America's elite junior players. There's no question that there's less discipline now than there was when I was on the Junior Davis Cup team in the early '60s. Then it was ruled with an iron fist. We were told how to behave, and we obeyed.
>
> Now the wunderkinder have a different attitude: "Want to throw your racket? Go ahead, it's OK. Want to slam a ball and cuss? Go ahead and do it. Just don't lose this match."
>
> Why? Because the rewards are enormous—a chance to be a multimillionaire before you're 21, to be on the cover of *Sports Illustrated* and *Newsweek* and *People*, to be surrounded 360 degrees by cameras after a big match.

Major junior tournaments offer much more than pure competition, not all of it good. It is at these tournaments that one is most likely to see kids throwing tantrums on the court while their parents and coaches throw tantrums in the stands; equipment representatives smoothly trying to convince the top juniors to use their sneakers, shorts, rackets, or string; promoters of other tournaments trying to entice players to their events with promises of airfare, hotel expenses, or other goodies; agents trying to line up prospective money winners; coaches jockeying to recruit the best players.

This side of competition is going to exist for the talented young player, but how he deals with it depends on the parent. Parents should ask themselves, "Are you carried away with the glamor of it all? Do you feel complimented by all the attention your child is getting? Do you tolerate bratty behavior from your talented wunderkind?" Parents can teach their child that regardless of his ranking, they expect nothing but the most polite and proper behavior from him on and off the court. Others may pamper a child—parents have no control over that—but they can make sure they don't. Parents can also help a child gain perspective on his situation. Fame is ephemeral and fickle and can be enjoyed for its momentary rewards. However, a child's self-esteem should not be linked to the number of people making a fuss over him or the number of news clippings about him. A child should be made to understand that being honest, ethical, moral, kind, and loving are the qualities that make a person good and decent, not being famous. This is not to say that your child should be penalized for attracting public attention, but he should always keep in mind his more substantial and long-lasting values.

Why a Child May Be Afraid to Compete

Generally, the main reason a child fears competition is extreme parental pressure. Without beating this point to death, suffice it to say that putting unnecessary pressure on a child is one of the most psychologically damaging things a parent can do to a child and to his relationship with his child.

Another principal reason for a child's fearing competition is meeting too much failure too soon. My brother's early tournament experience is a good example of just such a situation. Parents should take into careful consideration the skill level of their child and find a suitable level of competition for him. The child should not be put among kids who are far better, older, and bigger. Let a child start out slowly and meet with as much early success as possible.

Losses are bound to occur but can be dealt with constructively. One point that is important for a child to remember is that early losses are not necessarily a good indication of the child's potential. A child may be learning techniques that are hard to master now but will pay off when he is bigger and stronger. Tony Trabert never did win a national junior title at Kalamazoo, Michigan. Brian Gottfried won the national 12-and-under, but he didn't win another national tournament for seven years, when he won the national 18s.

If a child can learn to cope with losses constructively, competition should never become a frightening thing.

How Old Should a Child Be to Compete?

Competition is part of a child's tennis experience from the very beginning. In tennis lessons and in drills a child is taught to play little "games" that generally have the youngster competing against himself. These "games" are used to help a child learn and improve while making the process fun. In a typical lesson of Nick's you can hear . . .

Okay, honey, let's see how many forehands you can get over the net in a row. That's good, excellent. Okay, you got five shots over, now try to get seven.

In a very nonthreatening way, a child can be introduced to competition. It is then just a small step to competing against another person. Nick might instruct his pupil, "You can hit five balls in a row in a lesson; let's see if you can do that in every rally against this little boy." The child may lose the match, but Nick might say, "You did great! You kept the ball in play at least four shots every rally!" Competition can then be a fun and challenging part of a child's tennis. If competition is approached in this way, there really is no age that is too young or too old for a child to start competing. However, if a child starts in his teens, the competition may be fairly tough, which is the problem my brother ran into. In cases like this, the level of tournament entered should be chosen carefully, so the competition doesn't overwhelm the child.

Gains and Losses for Parents

Elements often overlooked by parents trying to do the best for their children are the overall gains and losses for the parents themselves. The following are some factors parents should take into consideration.

On the plus side is the satisfaction of seeing your child

strive to become good in something. The sadness of defeats is usually balanced by the happiness of wins, and watching your child mature by coping with losses has a satisfaction of its own. Helping your child pursue an activity he loves is an immeasurable joy.

Other gains for parents are the friendships they form. Tournaments take them out of their usual spheres of work and neighborhood, and place them in a new environment among people of varying backgrounds. Yet all these parents have one important common interest and have a common ground for communication.

Involvement and variety are other pluses. The atmosphere at tournaments is exciting, and parents soon collect favorites they like to cheer for. It's interesting to study the form and tactics of other players, see who's improving and who's not, and see how your child fares against the best. The scenarios are constantly changing, so your interest stays high and you find yourself emotionally involved, not only with your child but with others as well.

On the down side is the obvious aspect of money. Tony Trabert recalls:

> There's no question that my dad had to do some planning, because we didn't have much money. I remember when I was on the circuit, he used to borrow $1,000 from the bank in the summer and pay it back in the winter.

Even more demanding on her parents, in Billie Jean King's view, was the huge time investment they had to make. Because extra money was also a problem in her family, her father held down two jobs and her mother had one. So finding time to take their daughter to tournaments and their son to Little League was quite a trick. Billie Jean remembers those days.

> My parents were always tired and always trying to find time to take me places. Sometimes I could see they were really torn between making time for Randy and me and

our activities, and making time for themselves so they could rest.

Thus, money and time investments can be big disadvantages for parents.

Also on the minus side is the possibility of becoming overly involved. Sometimes you can want something for your child so much that it takes too much out of you. My mother would get so nervous during some of my matches that she would have to leave. Other mothers have different solutions. One day I was walking on the grounds of a tournament in England and ran into Lil Teeguarden, the mother of Pam Teeguarden, a high-ranking player on the women's tour. At that moment Pam was playing Evonne Goolagong on the stadium court and Lil was sitting by one of the outermost outside courts with her head in her lap and her hands over her ears. It turned out that she was so nervous about Pam's match that she didn't know what to do with herself. She couldn't stand watching, but she couldn't tear herself away from the courts either. Her solution was to sit as far away from the stadium as possible with her hands over her ears, so she couldn't hear the stadium announcer, and with her head in her lap, so she couldn't see the stadium scoreboard!

Overinvolvement can take uglier turns. One year, when I was playing the national 18s at the Philadelphia Cricket Club, the tournament had to hire Pinkerton guards to keep a certain father off the grounds. He had gotten so irate with another father that he had started a fist fight! Tony Trabert can remember equally unpleasant situations.

I can remember parents going around the tournament with a handful of bills trying to get bets on their son against the boy he was going to play. This kind of father would also get involved about line calls and officiating.

Thus, getting overly involved in their child's tournaments is a big minus for some parents. Not only do they make their own life unpleasant by getting too nervous, smoking too

237

much, drinking too much, and getting into arguments, but they probably make the child's life miserable as well.

Besides understanding these possible parental gains and losses, parents must realize other responsibilities they must assume if their child competes. Parents are responsible for how their child adapts to competition. Therefore, they must constantly monitor their own feelings and reactions as well as their child's. Monitoring doesn't mean analyzing and dissecting your behavior to the point of self-consciousness. It does mean regularly making an honest appraisal of your emotions and your child's. Are you enjoying tournaments? Is your child? Do you like the life-style? Do tournaments leave you too little time for other activities you enjoy? Do you resent giving your child so much time? Do your child's losses upset you too much? Do tournaments cause tension at home between you and your child? These questions and many more have to be asked and answered honestly. If problems arise, you can then be ready to deal with them promptly and effectively.

Monitoring your child's behavior and emotions means being ready to talk and *listen* to your child, and being alert to any meaningful nonverbal behavior. Discuss with your child how he feels about tournaments. Is competing fun? How does he or she feel after a win? a loss? Is it hard to play against friends? What makes him the most nervous? Does he feel pressured by anyone? By you? Is there anything he would like to see changed? What are his goals? Drawing your child out to discuss these matters is an art and won't be accomplished in one session, so be persistent. Your child can learn that it's okay to feel certain emotions and talk about them. It's okay to feel anxious, scared, disappointed, depressed, joyous, boastful, or afraid of disappointing you. In voicing his feelings to you, your child can feel that his emotions are legitimate and can be accepted by you, which makes it easier for your child to accept his own emotions.

Some nonverbal behavior can be just as telling as some discussions. Does your child seem nervous or afraid to tell you about losses? Does he get depressed by losses for days? Is your child biting his nails? losing sleep? not eating as well? being a bad sport on the court? If parents can notice these behaviors soon enough, many potential problems can be eliminated before they do any damage. If your child is going to compete, you should be ready and willing to increase your sensitivities to yourself and your child in order to dissipate any pressures that may arise. In openly discussing these pressures with your child, you can help your child develop a positive and healthy attitude about competition.

COMPETITION CAN be an extremely rewarding part of a child's tennis experience, but how rewarding this experience is depends on the parent. Win or lose, a child can deal with any result if his parents can deal with it. Having open and honest discussions regarding winning and losing is an important way for parents to convey to their child a healthy attitude about competition.

There are certain advantages and disadvantages to competition for both the young player and the parent, but the disadvantages can be nullified if the parent is aware, sensitive, and prepared. Competition is an irrefutable part of life. The tennis court is a perfect place for a child to learn about competition and how to deal with it constructively.

14.

All About Tournaments

If a child has decided to try to play in a tournament, what is the next step? In this chapter is all the information parents should have to get parent and child smoothly through the first few tournaments.

Finding a Tournament

The first thing a parent should do is check with his child's coach, his club, and the local public park system for any junior tournaments. With luck, there will be some tournaments just for novices—the best place for your child to start. If the competition is too easy, look for a tougher tournament next time, but meanwhile, the child has won a match or two.

The larger junior tournaments are listed by the U.S.T.A. sectional associations. (See Appendix for addresses of the sectional associations.) Write to the nearest sectional association and, for a small fee, they will send a schedule of tournaments in the area for the year. Most of the tournaments will come in the summertime, but a few will be played during the school year on weekends and during holidays.

Next, obtain entry forms from the sectional association, or write directly to the tournaments. Parent and child should fill out the entry form together with accurate information. The exact date of the child's birthday is important because it will determine whether he plays in the 10, 12, 14, 16, or 18-and-under age category. A child can always enter an older age group, but never a younger. If the form asks for past results and the child has some, be sure to include them. For this portion scores are usually asked, so keep an accurate record of the child's matches. Pay close attention to the deadline date for entries. It can be heartbreaking to a youngster if the form isn't sent in on time and he finds he is not entered in the tournament. When a child is very young, the responsibility for this paperwork lies with the parent, but even then the child's help should be enlisted. As a child gets older (13, 14, 15), more and more of the paperwork and the meeting of deadlines should be met by him. If children really want to play tournaments, they will be responsible and efficient in entering them.

The Draw

The draw, an ordered list of all the players in a child's event, is posted in a central area at the tournament. It is important that both parent and child learn to read a draw correctly because it tells who the child will play. The draw will also often indicate the place and time of the child's match. The most common type of draw is an elimination draw. In this draw, players are paired off to play each other with only the winner advancing to the next round. Thus, if you lose, you are eliminated entirely from that event. (Always check for consolation events where first- or second-round losers are eligible.) Another type of draw, used much less frequently, is the round robin. In a round robin each person plays every other person in the draw, and the player with the most total games is the winner. While the elimination draw is often used for events with 64, 96, 128 or more players, a round robin is used for tournaments with only 4, 6, or 8 players.

Seedings are important parts of elimination draws. Based on recent tournament results, the best players are "seeded," or ranked and distributed throughout the draw, in such a way that they wouldn't meet each other in early rounds. Depending on the size of a draw, either 2, 4, 6, 8, or 16 players can be seeded.

How to Choose a Doubles Partner

It is up to each player to find his own doubles partner. If a child is just starting out and doesn't know anyone, tell or write the tournament director about it. Someone else might be in the same predicament and the director can help bring the two players together. If a child does know someone to ask to play doubles, they should ask as soon as possible, before the other player commits himself to someone else. Everybody is different in what they consider important in choosing a doubles partner. Some people go for the best player, others for friends, and others for someone of similar ability. What was most important to me as a junior and remains topmost with me today is finding someone with a similar attitude on the court. My attitude in doubles is to try my heart out for every point but have fun doing it. If everything is grim and somber out there, I get too nervous, but if I can talk and joke with my partner occasionally I can stay loose and play better. Another extremely important quality to me is my partner's honesty. Not only do I not want to be associated with someone of dubious integrity, but I don't want to be embarrassed on the court by my partner's behavior and have to correct his calls. After these qualities have been met, I look for someone whose style of play complements mine. For example, if a child is a consistent player, he may look for someone with a knockout punch to close out the point. If a child has power but is erratic, he may do well with someone with less power but more consistency.

When a child first starts playing tournaments, finding a suitable doubles partner will take a lot of trial and error. Before too long he will become friendly with other players and learn what he likes and dislikes in a partner. Doubles is an extremely fun event in tournaments, being less pressured yet giving a child match experience. Children should be encouraged by parents to enter it.

Match Preparation

Match preparation is something parents can help their child with, but he should learn to take care of himself as soon as possible. A child will probably be playing many more matches without his parents' presence than with it, so the sooner a child takes responsibility for match preparation, the better.

A child should go to bed early the night before a match and get at least eight hours' sleep. If a child is hit with prematch jitters and spends a relatively sleepless night, it's important for him to realize that he can function beautifully on nervous energy. If he has been taking care of himself and getting his rest, one bad night isn't going to hurt him. Parents should not let their child psych himself out if he doesn't get a full night's sleep. If a child has an early morning match, parents must make sure he is awake for at least a few hours before match time. A child's body needs time to wake up fully before asking it to do something as demanding as playing a tournament match. For this reason, afternoon naps should be planned carefully. Naps are fine, but sometimes they can make a player groggier than before the nap, so allow plenty of time to wake up.

The next thing to consider on match day is when to eat. A meal should be eaten at least four hours before a match. If a child gets hungry between the meal and match time, a piece of fruit, a small salad, or a slice or two of toast can serve as snacks. If a child isn't hungry at all, he shouldn't be forced to have a meal. When I was a junior, before matches I had no appetite for breakfast and didn't eat a meal until after my match, yet had no lack of energy. For the child who doesn't want a meal, a glass of juice or milk, a slice of toast or a piece of fruit should supply ample energy. Pancho Gonzales liked the feeling of playing on an empty stomach. If he had a late evening match, he would have a light breakfast in the morning and, except for an orange or two, would not eat again until after his match, which might be around midnight. Food consumed too close to vigorous physical activity will tend to give the player a heavy, logy, sluggish, even nauseous feeling, and in fact will probably make him slower. On the other hand, going out on an empty stomach may only give the player a hunger pang or two. However, if a child feels any dizziness, at least a little food should be consumed. In general it's far better for a child to play on an empty stomach than on a full one.

On the day of a match, a child should allow time for stretching and warming up. About 15 minutes should be spent stretching and about 15 to 30 minutes hitting. This warm-up is just to get everything loosened up, so all strokes should be hit. It's good to break a sweat, but the player should not get tired. Exactly how much a child should warm up is an individual matter. Chris Evert likes to hit for 40 minutes and Billie Jean will hit for an hour or more, but Martina will hit for only around 15 or 20 minutes. How long a player warms up also depends on how close the warm-up is to match time. Some players like to go straight from the warm-up into the match; others like an hour or more in between. The child should experiment a little to find what suits him best. A prematch warm-up is definitely helpful in getting the kinks out and soothing flighty nerves.

If a child warms up on the tournament grounds, he should check in with the tournament desk before warming up. If he warms up elsewhere, he should check in upon arriving at the tournament site. Always check with the tournament desk first thing in case the schedule has been changed in any way. Tournaments generally have a 15-minute default rule, so a child can afford only to be 15 minutes late at the most. If a child wins, he should then inquire at the tournament desk for the time of his next match, which could be that day or the next. At no time should a child leave the grounds without informing the desk and making sure he has no more matches that day. The best habit a child can get into is always double checking his schedule.

Parental Responsibilities

Parents are responsible for getting their child to the tournament, having the child's desired meal or foods available, and making sure he has all the necessary supplies. Parents should take their child to the tournament in plenty of time for the child to check in, warm up, and maybe rest a bit. Be considerate of your child and don't be late or time your arrival so close that he feels rushed. Allow abundant time to drive to the tournament (especially if you've never been there before), park the car, and walk to the courts. When you begin to meet some parents from your neighborhood, you can form carpools and share the transportation chores. Parents should also double check to make certain their child has everything he will need. A typically equipped tournament player will have two rackets, balls, two sets of tennis clothes (one for singles and one for doubles), a warm-up suit, and dry clothes for the ride home. In a small "contingency kit," to be carried out to the court, some handy items to have are Band-aids, mole skin, adhesive tape, tincture of benzoin, aspirin, scissors, and extra sweatlets.

Away Tournaments

If a child would like to play a tournament away from home, housing and transportation around the tournament site are usually provided. These options are indicated on the entry form. Housing is generally supplied to all players who live more than forty or fifty miles away from the tournament. It is an amenity offered to the players but rarely to their parents. If parents want to accompany their child to an away tournament, there are several housing options. They can both stay with friends or in a hotel, or the child can stay with housing and the parents can stay with friends or in a hotel. Occasionally a tournament can supply housing for both a child and parent, but this is rare.

The families with whom a child will house are generally members of the host club, active in the local tennis community, or parents of other players. These families are carefully screened by the tournament so that unpleasant occurrences rarely happen. Most often, if anything unpleasant happens, it is usually because the guest player has been ill mannered or inconsiderate. Your child's hosts will assume supervision of your child in your absence, supply all meals, and provide local transportation. Often tournaments will offer players lunches and transportation to take some of the burden off the hosts.

The beauty of this housing arrangement is that a child can play tournaments away from home even if his parents do not have the time to take him. Parents, in turn, can feel secure in knowing that their child is well supervised. All they basically have to do is arrange for transportation for their child between home and the tournament.

Responsibilities of a Player as a Houseguest

While maintaining his tennis discipline as much as possible, a child's first responsibility is to blend in with the host's family. This includes going to bed and waking up at times that are convenient for the child as well as the host. A child should help out with the daily chores so that he is as little a burden to the host as possible. Making his own bed, keeping the bedroom neat, helping with meals and dishes are all chores a child can do easily. A child should be considerate and try to let the host know where he will be at all times and the time of all his matches. At the end of the tournament many houseguests like to give their hosts a small gift of appreciation, and a thank-you note should always be written. Families who volunteer to house players are willing to donate extra time and effort to make their guest's stay pleasant and successful. With a little sensitivity and consideration, a child can make the job easy for his hosts and be a welcomed guest next year.

Parent Etiquette

For the most part, the less noticeable parents are at tournaments, the better. Tony Trabert appreciated his father's conduct at matches.

With my own children I like to do what my father did—you know, he was glad to be there, but he let me fight my

246

own battles. He would just sit quietly in the stands, watch and analyze.

When Ben Testerman was asked if there was anything he would like changed about the junior circuit, he said, "Yeah, I'd like to see more kids with coaches and without parents." Unfortunately, at junior tournaments the situation exists where a few bad eggs give the group a bad name. Helping and supporting a child is fine, but hovering over and making decisions for him deprives a child of learning how to be self-sufficient. Also, children with doting, interfering parents are looked down upon by other children. To make it easier on a child, parents should be there for moral support but be inconspicuous.

Where a parent sits for his child's match is an obvious feature of how conspicuous a parent can be. At some small tournaments the only place to sit is right on the court. This is okay, but a parent will then have to be as stoic as possible. As Mrs. Austin said, "One of the hardest things for me at Tracy's matches is sitting there smiling." If a parent is going to sit right on the court, he can't go wild clapping for his child or groan at a miss, not only because it might bother the other player but because it might even bother his own child. A player may get embarrassed by a parent's overt partisanship. Even on their best behavior, parents can accidentally bother their children. My mother was sitting on the court during a tough 14-and-under match of mine. As usual, she was wearing stockings. Every time I missed or came close to missing a shot, my mother would cross or uncross her legs. Unnoticed by her, but louder than a bomb to me, was the sound of her stockings rubbing against each other when she would cross her legs. So even before a rally was over, I'd know by the sound of her stockings which shots she thought I wouldn't get. Without realizing it at all, my mother had created quite a distraction for me. I won that day, but I asked her not to wear stockings to any more of my matches.

Another disadvantage to parents' sitting on the court is how it reflects on their child to the other players. When I

247

was a junior and saw a parent on the court when there was other seating available, I would think, "Oh, one of *those* parents," meaning pushy, interfering parents. "Those parents" would sit and write down the score to make sure their child didn't get cheated, stand up and object to line calls, and generally be a nuisance. To avoid being or looking like one of "those parents," mothers and fathers shouldn't sit on the court unless they have to.

The best place for parents to sit is up in the stands with everyone else. They can be supportive and clap for their child when it's appropriate, but shouldn't embarrass him by being a noisy, rowdy fan. It's difficult trying to be so controlled when you feel so involved with one person, but it reflects better on both parent and child.

Another point of parent etiquette is not to intervene in a child's matches. The temptation for parents may be great when they think their child is being taken advantage of by another, but a child has to fight his own battles. First of all, it is only a parent's *opinion* that his child is being abused. In his partisan fervor, a parent may see things that don't really exist. Second, a child has to learn eventually to handle himself in tough situations. Yes, he may be getting pushed around this match, but the experience may serve as an invaluable lesson that will be helpful in future ones. When the child comes off the court, the parent can discuss the events and the possible actions the child could have taken and what he might do next time. If one child's parents involve themselves in the match, the best recourse is for the other child's parents to go directly to the tournament officials, and not get involved in a confrontation with another parent. A child should know that his parents are there to help, but also that they are going to go through the proper channels.

The only time a parent has a legitimate right to interfere in a match is when his child is misbehaving. We totally support taking a child off the court if he misbehaves, just as Mr. Pasarell did with his son Charlie. Parents should have discussions with their child, warning him of their actions, if they are necessary. If these actions become necessary, parents must follow through. It may be painful for parent and child, but it is effective and worthwhile. No match is more important than teaching a child sportsmanship and morality. An important aspect of a parent's presence at a tournament is how he reacts to the child's loss. Parents should be there to give comfort and consolation and a big hug when their child comes off the court. There really isn't anything a parent can say except that he loves the child. Give the child time to cool off emotionally before talking about the match. At this point parents can be helpful by asking some constructive questions that will help the child focus on his mistakes. If the child's coach is present, he should discuss the match with the child. That will eliminate a parent's becoming the target of any of the child's residual bad feelings from the match. It's a parent's duty to be loving, not to be a demanding coach.

TOURNAMENTS NEED not be bewildering or frightening for the novice player if both the child and parent are somewhat familiar with the general procedures. The most important aspect for the parent at tournaments is to plan his time well so the child is ready, punctual, and unrushed for matches. Being supportive and comforting but noninterfering is another important parental obligation.

Tournaments provide a child with an opportunity to travel, be self-sufficient, and learn to be a welcomed houseguest. Match preparation can teach a child to plan his time, form a routine, and take care of himself for optimum performance. Win or lose, the experience a child can gain from tournaments will make him a winner.

15.

Lessons in Life

It should have become apparent to the reader that this book is not just about tennis. The principles discussed can be applied to any sport or activity. How a parent should relate to a young tennis player is similar to how a parent should relate to a young swimmer, dancer, or violinist. How a parent and child relate regarding an activity, and how the child expresses himself through the activity, affects not only that specific activity but every other endeavor the child attempts. Thus, tennis is not an entity apart from real life. In many ways it *is* real life and mirrors a child's personality, morality, and character.

Knowing One's Self

Tennis can help a child establish a sense of identity. Children like to be something special. They like to identify themselves with groups in order to define their own identities. Being a boy or a girl, sister or brother, or student is nothing special in a child's eye. Being a tennis player along with these other features is adding something different, something special, and starts to give that child a feeling of being totally unique. This process is one way a person starts to establish a feeling of having an individual identity separate from parents, siblings, or anyone else.

More important, the child soon learns that he is many things besides just a tennis player. Tennis is not his complete identity; how he scores in a tennis game doesn't define his total personality, just part of it. Thus, tennis can help form a child's feelings of self-identity and self-esteem, but not dominate them. A child may learn to think: "I'm a person who plays tennis, but I'm also many other things. Winning or losing a tennis game doesn't mean I'm a winner or loser in life. The *way* I play the game, not the score, can make me a winner."

Value Systems

A by-product of a child's going through these thinking processes is that they help him develop a value system. If winning or losing is not top priority, what is? Your child can learn that important values in tennis and in life are being fair and just, giving a full effort, trying for excellence, and rebounding from setbacks.

If a child has a clear understanding of his value system and priorities and lives up to them, he acquires a sense of high self-esteem. A boy is uncoordinated and plays a dismal game of tennis but approaches the game with 100 percent effort and concentration and displays impeccable sportsmanship. If that boy is raised to believe that effort and sportsmanship are far more important than winning, and is rewarded for them, he will undoubtedly feel good about himself. He has self-worth, self-esteem.

This is how tennis can be a learning vehicle in the formation of a child's character. Through tennis he can develop a sense of self, a value system, and a feeling of high self-esteem.

Lessons in Morality

The principles of right and wrong that a child learns on a tennis court are the principles he will utilize in life. There is very little difference between cheating on a tennis court, cheating on a school exam, or cheating on an income tax return. A person who stretches the rules on a tennis court will stretch them at the office, at home, at church. A person who cheats in tennis will cheat in other areas of his life; the pattern is the same, only the activity changes.

251

Through tennis a child can learn that there are certain rules in life that must be obeyed and standards that must be upheld. In tennis the rules are extremely explicit, and obeying them is fairly simple. If a child can call a crucial point correctly in favor of his opponent, then he can more easily learn to make other, more difficult moral decisions. For example, a teen-ager puts a dent in a parked car (without any damage to his own car) in a dark and empty parking lot. What is it that leads the youngster to do the right thing and leave a note, or do the wrong thing and run away? Tennis offers a child the opportunity to learn to do the right thing under pressure—lessons that a child will benefit from in every other area of life. Frank Boyden, headmaster of Deerfield Academy for sixty-six years, said, "The consequence of poor sportsmanship is that you lose somewhere along the line." Conversely, the consequence of good sportsmanship is that you win somewhere along the line.

Lessons in Coping

To play tennis is to learn to cope with life. On the tennis court a player has to cope with tension, mistakes, pressure, injury, winning, losing, fear, and excitement. Tennis teaches a child to cope with these features of life in many ways.

Probably one of the first things a young player learns is to admit and accept his mistakes—it's almost unavoidable. If the ball goes out, there's no one else around to blame. A young player can discover that by admitting his mistakes and accepting them, he can then go about correcting them. In this way mistakes are a useful part of the learning process—not totally negative, frightening occurrences. A child will commit many mistakes in different areas all his life. It is far better that he learn how to cope with them early on a tennis court.

A young player learns to cope with the difficulties of pressure. Whether the child is playing a big tournament match, a school ladder event, or just a game he would like to win out of pride, the youngster experiences pressure. The child discovers that the best way to cope with pressure is to be totally prepared, take one thing at a time, stay in the here and now, and not confuse excitement with fear. These methods of coping can then be transferred to other pressure situations in the child's life. What better way to face final exams at school than to know the material thoroughly, tackle one course and one exam at a time, not worry about one exam while studying for another, and interpret nervous energy as excitement about taking exams, not fear? What better way to deal with a tough job assignment? speech? driver's test? or any number of situations that are challenging, yet scary at first?

In addition, a child can learn to cope with the desire to improve, to progress. He learns this in school, but the lesson is more easily learned on the court, where goals are not so obscure and the results more visible. A child acquires the knowledge that by setting short-term goals, long-term goals can be secured. "If I practice my backhand a lot this week, next month I might beat so-and-so." "Through hard practice this year, I might make the school team next year." This pattern of reasoning can then lead to, "If I do my homework today, I can do well on the exam next week." Or, "If I want to get into a good college, I have to do well in school this year and next." Thus, to improve in anything in life, the child learns to set reasonable goals and methodically try to attain each one.

Lessons in Competition

Competition in tennis adds another dimension to the lessons in life a child can learn. Competition is an unavoidable element of life. In the most fundamental sense, our very survival is based on competition. With competition, then, being a fact of life, it is better to meet it head on and acquire the necessary knowledge to cope with it. Tennis provides a safe atmosphere in which a child can learn about competition. What a child has already begun to learn in playing noncompetitive tennis now becomes more and more magnified. Morality becomes an even bigger issue. In competition a child's sportsmanship is put to the test—emotions are at a higher pitch, the temptations greater. If a child can learn to deal with these inner pressures on the tennis court with good sportsmanship and dignity, then he will have a great head start in life. Despite any faults Jimmy Connors may have, on several occasions he has reversed a linesman's call, to favor his opponent. Some people claim he has even lost an extremely important and lucrative match because of this behavior. To be moral under such circumstances is to be moral indeed.

Competition can teach a child that his self-esteem is not based on results or scores. Winning or losing a tennis match doesn't make someone an inherently better or worse person. What is of value and what does affect a child's self-esteem is the *process* of playing, which includes such qualities as full effort and sportsmanship. If children feel they have played the game in the best way they know, in the long run they will feel good about themselves despite the score outcome. The problem for both children and adults is keeping a clear separation between process and outcome.

If this separation between process and outcome can be made, and kept in mind, then success and failure can be treated for what they are—transitory states. A child will neither get carried away by success nor completely demoralized by failure. Approached in the right way, competition can teach humility and modesty in the face of success, and strength and resiliency in the face of failure—lessons to help a child cope with any success or failure later in life.

Competition brings out the excellence in a child, thereby teaching him how to bring it out in himself. Competition motivates the child to plan, work hard, and strive to excel. Eventually the child realizes that to strive for excellence is in itself rewarding, even without the added motivation of competition. At first the child wants to improve his backhand in order to beat an opponent. Gradually, the child realizes that it is fun to improve, and seeing progress in oneself is reward enough. Studying for a good grade turns into studying hard for the rewards of learning and self-improvement. In seeking the advice of a lawyer, would you choose someone who practices for the money, or someone who practices because they love the law? The answer is obvious. Competition helps a child learn to strive for excellence and appreciate the rewards of self-improvement.

In addition, attempting to achieve excellence teaches the value of short-term "sacrifices" in the attainment of long-term gains. Part of being a child is to be short-sighted and want instant gratification, a quality that is also a major feature of immaturity in adults. Competition can teach the benefits of delaying gratification. A child learns that tonight's party will have to be missed to prepare for tomorrow's match, in order to reap the benefits of playing well. In the same way, later in life, a child may know that not spending money today for a new motorbike will leave more money next year to buy a new car. Life is full of trade-offs, and competition teaches your child to use foresight in choosing among alternatives.

Finally, with the experience of competing and dealing with the associated pressure comes the fringe benefit of learning to relax more and more in such situations. At first, playing in front of five people scared the daylights out of me, then I played before fifteen people, then fifty, two hundred, two thousand, then ten thousand—to the point now that audiences really don't make me nervous. I'm nervous all right, but not because of an audience (which I've blocked out of my mind) but because of the importance of the match to me. There are certain situations and audiences I'll never get used to totally, like the stadium courts at Wimbledon and Flushing Meadow, but I get better at calming myself with each appearance. Having these "frightening" tennis experiences has helped me function well in other pressure-cooker situations. For example, how well I play tennis had nothing to do with how good a psychology student I was, yet when the time came for me to defend orally my Ph.D. dissertation to my doctoral committee I soothed my nerves by thinking, "I've performed in a stadium filled with thousands of people; what's so nerve racking about talking to six people in a little room?" The two events were totally unrelated, yet the knowledge that I had coped with a lot of pressure in a previous situation gave me confidence in my present situation.

Thus, tennis is not an isolated event in a child's life. It contains the ingredients to help a child deal successfully with all aspects of life in the present and in the future as an adult. We hope we have provided parents with much practical information to help them get their child involved in tennis in the right way. We also hope we have stimulated parents to think about the ways in which they can help their child deal with tennis experiences in a psychologically beneficial way. Tennis in a child's life can be at least partially responsible for a physically and psychologically healthy life, and a fulfilling relationship between parent and child.

Appendices

U.S.T.A. Sectional Associations

Eastern Tennis Association
180 E. Post Road
Room 207
White Plains, N.Y. 10601

Florida Tennis Association
520 N.E. 118 Street
Biscayne Park, Fla. 33161
Helen Darress

Hawaii Tennis Association
Box 411
Honolulu, Hawaii 96815
Bobbie Barton

Intermountain Tennis Association
Box 6740
Denver, Colo. 80206
Gilbert F. Roberts

Middle Atlantic Tennis Association
5656 Ravenel Lane
Springfield, Va. 22151
Unni MacDonald

Middle States Tennis Association
Love Road
RD 1, Box 146
Reading, Pa. 19601
Susie Lee

Missouri Valley Tennis Association
5727 Manchester
St. Louis, Mo. 63110
Fern Soxman

New England Lawn Tennis Association
Box 223
Needham, Mass. 02192

Northern California Tennis Association
Box 337
Moraga, Ca. 94556

Northwestern Tennis Association
3769 Towndale Drive
Bloomington, Minn. 55431
Rosemary Rockwell

Pacific Northwest Tennis Association
Box 130
Gresham, Ore. 97030
Harold Parrott

Puerto Rico Lawn Tennis Association
Box 40456
Minillas Station
Santurce, Puerto Rico 00940

Southern California Tennis Association
609 N. Cahuenga Boulevard
Los Angeles, Calif. 90004

Southern Tennis Association
3121 Maple Drive
N.E. Room 21B
Atlanta, Ga. 30305

Southwestern Tennis Association
1735 Rite NE
Albuquerque, N.M. 87106
Jeanne Brummell

Texas Tennis Association
Box 192
Austin, Tex. 78767
Ben T. Ball

Western Tennis Association
1024 Torrence Drive
Springfield, Ohio 45505
Mrs. Bernard Schubert

Suggestions for Further Reading

Food for Fitness. Editors of *Runner's World* Magazine. Mountain View, California: World Publications, 1976.

Glover, B. & Shepherd, J. *The Runner's Handbook*. New York: Penguin Books, 1978.

Greene, Robert Ford. *Tennis Drills*. New York: Hawthorne Books, Inc., 1976.

Hittleman, R. L. *The Yoga Way*. New York: Avon Books, 1978.

Maltz, Maxwell. *Psycho-Cybernetics*. Hollywood, California: Wilshire Book Company, 1971.

Pritikin, Nathan. *The Pritikin Program for Diet and Exercise*. New York: Grosset & Dunlap, 1979.

INDEX

Achilles' tendinitis, 74
Achilles' tendon strain, 45
affluent parents, 96–99
age
 of beginning tennis, 6–7
 endurance and, 48
 groupings in junior programs, 8
 selection of tournaments, 240
Aitchison, Alex, 196
amino acids, 62
Anthony, Gary, 226–27
arch support, 75
Arias, Jimmy, 219
Ashe, Arthur, 26, 51, 84, 151, 189, 215, 233
Association for Intercollegiate Athletics for Women (A.I.A.W.), 220
atherosclerosis, 64
Austin, Jeanne, 20–21, 131, 138, 195, 196, 197, 209, 210
Austin, Tracy, 6, 20–21, 84, 98, 131, 138, 178, 197, 209–10, 219, 232

backaches, 43–44
backboards, 82–83
Bartkowicz, Peaches, 178–79
blisters, 38–39, 74
Bodo, Peter, 21, 193
Borg, Bjorn, 70, 84, 98, 189, 193, 195, 205
Boyden, Frank, 252
Brandy, Josito, 32–33
breathing, relaxation and, 151
Bundy, May Sutton, 100, 131

carbohydrate metabolism, fats and, 64
cardiovascular disease, 63
cardiovascular training, 48–49
Casabianca, Claudia, 200
Casals, Rosie, 51, 100
Cawley, Evonne Goolagong, 49, 237
Cawley, Roger, 83
character building, 151–52, 250–56
 See also personality formation
cheating, 97, 190–91, 196–98, 202
choking, 146–47
cholesterol, 64
clothing, 43, 77–79, 98–99

coaches
 certification of, 134
 and college admission, 223–24
 relationship with parents, 132–34
 responsibilities of, 10–11
 role of, 128
 selection of, 88, 129–31, 134–35
 at tournament, 249
 See also coaching; parent–coach relationship
coaching
 amount required, 135–36
 and coach–student relationship, 129–31
 and college selection for tennis, 221
 coping with pressure and, 148–52
 cost of, 98
 free, 100
 and mental attitude, 140–42
 by parents, 137–39
college, tennis and, 217, 219–22
competition
 benefits of, 227–29
 disadvantages of, 229–34
 eating before, 61–62
 emotions and, 191–93
 fear of, 234–35
 and handicapped children, 34
 social benefits of, 229
 tennis and lessons in, 253–56
 See also tournaments
Connors, Gloria, 137
Connors, Jimmy, 6, 78, 137, 195, 212
coping, tennis and, 252–53
cost(s)
 of coaching, 98, 136–37
 of competition, 236
 court fees, 85
 of equipment, 70–72, 81
 of junior programs at clubs, 87
 for serious tennis player ages ten to eighteen, 101–3
 of tennis balls, 79
 of tennis shoes, 75
 See also financial aid
Court, Margaret, 13–14
courts, 80–81
 See also tennis-playing locations

260